D0975664

The Attic

The Attic

Memoir of a Chinese Landlord's Son

GUANLONG CAO

Translated by Guanlong Cao and Nancy Moskin

UNIVERSITY OF CALIFORNIA PRESS

Berkeley   Los Angeles   London

To my father and mother,
who are no longer here
to read this book

University of California Press
Berkeley and Los Angeles, California

University of California Press, Ltd.
London, England

© 1996 by
The Regents of the University of California

Library of Congress Cataloging-in-Publication Data

Ts' ao, Kuan-lung, 1945–
    The attic : memoir of a Chinese landlord's son / Guanlong Cao ;
translated by Guanlong Cao and Nancy Moskin.
        p.   cm.
    Translation from Chinese.
    ISBN 0-520-20405-0 (alk. paper)
    I. Title.
PL2912.A5335A77 1996
951.05'092—dc20
    [B]   95-38541
                                                  CIP

Printed in the United States of America
9 8 7 6 5 4 3 2 1

Acknowledgments

Special thanks to my friend Nancy Moskin for her close collaboration and significant contribution to the entire process of translation, rewriting, and editing this book. Her creativity and hard work are integrated into every page.

Much appreciation goes to my friend Sas Carey for her great support and encouragement when I wrote the first draft in Middlebury, Vermont.

My gratitude to Sheila Levine, my editor, for her faith in this book.

I'd also like to thank the people who generously contributed their critiques and suggestions. They are Jean Arrowsmith, Rey Chow, Virginia Earle, Larry Johnson, Lynn and J. Robert Moskin, Doris Moskin, Monica Raymond, Richard Strassberg, and Lauraine and George Warfield.

Last, but chronologically first, I am grateful to Professor Perry Link at Princeton University and Professor John Berninghausen at Middlebury College, who introduced my earlier writings to the United States. Without their efforts, the change in my life described in the last chapter of this book would never have happened.

Contents

Memory of the Belly / 1

The Bodhisattva's Toes / 7

Bath / 11

The Penglai Market / 16

The Temple of Letters / 21

Anecdotes About the Roof / 29

Going to the Great World / 37

Taxi Hopping / 43

Sizzling Grease / 49

Pigs' Heads / 54

Sheep Fat Soap / 61

Rotten Fruit / 65

Father Was Old / 71

Crystal Radio / 76

The Culture of Killing / 84

The Milk Incident / 97

Relocation / 101

Automotive School / 112

Mr. Lu / 119

The Pursuit of Oil / 126

Chopsticks / 130

Sweet Potatoes / 135

Dentist Herb / 141

Bean Dregs Paste / 148

Wet Dream / 153

Shovel-Shaped Fences / 157

Bao Changed / 163

The Sadness of the Phoenix Fish / 169

Travel Pass and Wheat Flour / 175

Cricoid Cartilage / 185

Rubber Plantation / 197

My Injury / 208

I Am Hunted / 216

No Armband / 227

I Slapped My Sister / 232

Farewell / 241

CHAPTER ONE

Memory of the Belly

I slept in the same bed as my mother until I was seven years old.

That was more than forty years ago, in the early 1950s, in Shanghai.

My mother was full and fair, with thin eyes and thin eyebrows, a little like palace ladies in Tang dynasty paintings. Mother seldom smiled, but when she did, her smile was charming—her teeth even and white. Mother had a full head of luxuriant hair. It was so shiny that if she ever had the chance to stroll down Manhattan's Fifth Avenue, I am sure the fashionable New York girls would have approached her for the name of the fancy shampoo she used.

Mother, however, would not spend money on soap to wash her hair. Instead, she scrounged straw bags from the marketplace and burned them to ashes. When she wanted to wash her hair, Mother scooped a cupful of ash into a small pouch and soaked it in a big pot of warm water. Light gray trails seeped out of the pouch, dyeing the water the color of Wulong tea. Mother said ash contains soda, and soda is a good detergent.

When the special solution was ready, Mother poured her hair into the pot. She rubbed, twisted, and squeezed it, torturing the hair to her heart's content. But after rinsing, the hair was still as silky and alive as ever. And it left a whiff of the straw's ash behind, making her smallest son dream of the soda-tinged fragrance of reed-wrapped rice.

I said I slept in the same bed as my mother, but, in fact, there was no bed in our home. My family lived in an attic. The two slanted roofs and the floor formed an equilateral triangle—no bed could fit into that compact geometric shape. But the two sharp angles created spaces ideal for pallets. A large dormer window projected from each roof slope. The pallet under the northern window was for Father and my two older brothers, Bao and Ling. Mother, my younger sister, Chuen, and I used the one under the southern window. Six members of my family lived in this cozy nest, far from our homeland, quietly enjoying the time heaven graciously granted to us.

My father was originally from Jiangxi Province. He was the third son of a farmer who had lived beside Poyang Lake. Third sons in Chinese fairy tales are always a bit odd. So was my father. Father could easily have stayed with the foot-bound wife chosen for him by his parents, worked the small plot of land inherited from his ancestors, peacefully enjoyed his life, and peacefully been buried in his homeland.

He, however, chose to stir up his lukewarm life and tried his hand at a variety of businesses. Fortunately or unfortunately, his luck ran hot and he made some money. He bought a few acres of farmland and remarried, this time to a woman with big feet who became my mother. Four children were born to them. We moved to Shanghai when the Communist Revolution came. From that time on, Father spent his life, thirty declining years, in the attic.

My mother was the oldest daughter in her family. Her father had established a soap factory in Hunan Province. At eighteen, she had married a handsome officer from the local army. A couple of years after the wedding, she discovered her husband's insatiable whoring, and she went home to her parents. The officer tried to bring her back, but she never returned. She lived in her parents' house until her husband was killed in a battle in Jiangxi. Then, at thirty, my mother married my father.

Mother did not tell us about that part of her life until I was grown up and had to fill out an official *curriculum vitae,* a periodically updated biographical report. In order that her child could be truthful to the government, she briefly related her history. I was shocked.

When I think back, it seems I never saw Mother and Father sleep together. I never even saw any intimate behavior between them. In the minds of their four children, Mother and Father were eternally asexual. Their function was to raise the little creatures that came from nowhere, giving them food, giving them clothes, and, occasionally, giving them a good beating.

Mother belonged to me.

Her hair, with its fragrance of soda, belonged to me. Her back, her breasts, her tummy, even the sweat oozing from her body in summer, all of them belonged to me.

My sister, Chuen, is six years younger than I am. When I was seven, she was only one. Mother, in her sleep, always held Chuen and turned her back to me, but that by no means prevented me from possessing her.

There is a fish called the remora, which lives in the sea. Remoras have suction cups on their abdomens. The fish attach themselves to the backs of whales and hang on. The whale can never get rid of them, nor could my mother get rid of me.

Every night I hung on Mom's back. Her back was soft, without any bones. One of my hands would trespass around Mother's waist to hold her even softer belly.

Fat, soft, smooth, and warm, Mother's belly concentrated all the feminine charms. While cradling my sister, Mother bent her legs, creating rolls of flesh at her tummy, just for my little hand to squeeze and squeeze. Mother always tolerated me. No matter how I tormented her belly, even when I dug my fingers into her belly button, she tolerated me.

After I had mangled her tummy for a while, I would invade upward.

Being skinny is fashionable nowadays. Chests as flat as airport runways frequently require colorful patches to signal their precise coordinates. Mother never wore a bra because she had voluptuous breasts. I approached them in the dark and I never missed my landing zone.

The diameter and weight of her breasts far surpassed those of the rolls at her stomach. My fingers tired after a few forays. Then I would rest my hand between her breasts, letting the palm and back of my hand sleepily absorb my mother's warmth.

Sometimes my body would make a rhythmic movement. My stomach pressed repeatedly against Mother's behind. A kind of warm and swollen feeling would emanate from between my legs.

In those days I still occasionally wet the bed, but Mother never yelled at me or even made a fuss. In the morning when she got up, she would put a hot water bottle on the sheet where I had peed. Steam would arise, mixed with a faint smell of urine. My two brothers could probably smell it, but I never felt embarrassed. Chuen was younger than I and had not yet learned to defend herself. She had no alibi. She was my natural scapegoat.

But Mother was vigilant about the territory below her navel. Occasionally my little hand would probe downward. As soon as I touched a hair, my hand would be caught and escorted back to her tummy. I thought those hairs must be like the whiskers of a cat, remaining highly sensitive even when the cat is sleeping.

While wandering about Mother's body, my fingers frequently encountered my sister's tiny hands and tiny feet. But there was never any conflict. Sometimes Chuen put my fingers in her mouth and sucked on them. Nothing would come out, so she began to bite them with her pointed teeth. It hurt slightly, but only enough to register a few blips on my sleepy brain waves. So my sister and I shared Mother's love and maintained a harmonious coexistence. From those experiences, I presume, developed the bittersweet relationship Chuen and I shared when we were grown.

After my seventh birthday, for some unknown, or at least undeclared, reason, Mother exiled me to the northern reaches of the attic. Each night four males crowded onto a pallet like a well-laid-out dress pattern. Heads and feet interlocked in a complex arrangement. At midnight, if someone wanted to pee, he first had to dig himself out by moving a few legs and arms aside, and then had to be careful not to step on anybody's face.

For the first several nights I cried shamelessly. I cried to go back to Mommy's bed. My two brothers laughed at me, but I didn't care. The only problem was that every time I began to cry, Mother started to snore, and my noise-making instantly lost momentum. Like a baby being weaned, I took more than a week to adjust to my new status.

CHAPTER TWO

The Bodhisattva's Toes

Feet are very difficult to draw. I studied art at Middlebury College for four years, but even now, when I draw the human figure, I still tend to add some object from out of the blue to hide the toes of the model.

Comparative art history always assumes that classical Chinese painting emphasizes spirit rather than likeness. Human anatomy, it seems, was never in the curriculum for classical Chinese painters. But the realistic strokes of the portrait of the Bodhisattva in our attic mystically aroused the first pink fantasy in a boy's green mind.

For several hundred years Chinese women had their feet bound into three-inch-long "golden lotuses." These and their diminutive "cherry mouths," the merciless classical standards of beauty, pinched women for generation after generation like a pair of pliers. Although Lady Bodhisattva traveled through China as a missionary for many, many years, her Indian visa must have remained valid, providing immunity for her wandering, natural feet.

Our picture of the Bodhisattva was glued to the eastern wall of the attic. Before the revolution the ground floor of our building had housed an herbal pharmacy named Heaven. The attic had served as Heaven's upstairs stockroom. The four borders of the portrait were filled with all kinds of marks: dates, figures, names, and addresses. It seemed the Bodhisattva had worked as Heaven's accountant. When my family moved into the attic, Mother tore off all the yellowed wallpaper but did not disturb Lady Bodhisattva.

The picture was a woodcut print and included an advertisement for Dragon and Tiger Balm at the bottom. The Bodhisattva's healing powers encompassed everything from headaches to infertility, and the same was claimed for the balm.

The paper had absorbed moisture from the limestone wall behind, causing a layer of saltpeter needles to penetrate the picture, graying the shiny hair of the Bodhisattva—even a divine goddess could not escape secular aging. Luckily, her bare feet remained alluringly young.

The Bodhisattva stood on a white lotus flower floating in the water. She held a feather duster in her left hand, and a porcelain vase in her right. Her long gown poured down from her waist and the drapery splashed around her feet. In the ripples swam her pink toes.

When I say that her toes swam, I am not being merely rhetorical. Whenever I was left at home alone with my schoolwork, my mind wandered. I would cup my head in my hands and gaze at the toes of the goddess. Yes, those toes were really swimming, swimming away from the picture to somewhere between my legs under the table. And a faint pulsation would begin.

I remember once around New Year's, my mother brought her four children to the Town Gods' Temple. There were many statues of deities in the main hall. At every new year and on major festival days believers made offerings such as red silk capes, crackers, cakes, and fruits for the gods to enjoy.

On that day I saw an old woman carefully place a box in front of Lady Bodhisattva. We were curious about the contents of the gilded carton. The old woman lifted the lid and removed a pair of red shoes. They were narrow and pointed, in a style fashionable in those days. She put them right beneath the goddess's feet. I felt terrible imagining the woman pushing Lady Bodhisattva's soft, fleshy feet into those tight shoes. The shoes Mother made for me were as round as birds' nests, but every time I put on a new pair, my toes were pinched.

"Damn!" I let out a loud curse.

"No swearing in front of Lady Bodhisattva!" Mother rapped me on the top of my head.

Here it came again. Mother was really silly sometimes. Since there was a Bodhisattva in our house, Mother frequently used the deity to discipline me.

You say I'm not allowed to swear in front of the Bodhisattva, so how come Father always beats me in front of her when she cries if even an ant is hurt? And you, Mom, how can you chop pork into tiny pieces every day, right under the nose of a vegetarian goddess, and deep fry them until the attic is filled with greasy smoke?

I believed that as long as you were a good kid, it was not

necessary to butter up the Bodhisattva. If you were a bad kid, praying every day or singing hymns from dawn to dusk would not help.

I knew it was hard to be a monk. You cannot eat meat; you cannot return home; you cannot take a wife. But I thought that if Lady Bodhisattva was kind enough to take me as her little apprentice, I would happily give up all those things. Not eating meat would be fine; not returning home would be fine; not taking a wife would be fine. I didn't hope to enter heaven, and I didn't hope to be a big cadre or a millionaire in my next life. I only hoped that Lady Bodhisattva would allow me to be her little apprentice forever.

But what could a little apprentice do?

Well, I could wash feet, I could wash the Bodhisattva's feet.

CHAPTER THREE

Bath

Maybe it was some kind of compensation that, shortly after Mother kicked me out of her bed, I acquired my first girlfriend. Her name was Wang Tian. She was a classmate of mine. I was in second grade; she was in second grade, too. I was eight; she was eighteen.

Wang Tian's mother worked as a live-in maid for a family in Penglai Lane. Penglai Lane was only a few doors from my house. When I sat on the slanted roof outside our attic window, I often saw Wang Tian's mother sitting on her balcony, bent over a wooden tub, washing piles of laundry. Wang Tian and her mother lived in their employer's house. Wang Tian came to our attic often, but she never invited me to her home.

Wang Tian had large, shiny eyes. Each of her eyes seemed to have a strong will of its own. Sometimes they would head off in unsynchronized directions. This gave her face a trance-like expression as if she had just stepped off a cloud.

At that time the schools had started using Mandarin as the

official teaching language, but Wang Tian's country accent was hard to correct. Every time we sang *The Dawn of the East,* the hymn to Chairman Mao, and came to the line *"Where the sun shines, everything thrives,"* her hayseed accent would make it come out like *"Where the sun shines, every scar glitters,"* and laughter would erupt from the class.

The teacher, standing behind the podium, tried very hard to correct Wang Tian's pronunciation, but to little effect. Eventually, whenever we came to "Where the sun shines . . ." the teacher would raise his arm and point at Wang Tian, and her enthusiastic voice would immediately be muted.

However, Wang Tian's work on the abacus was excellent. When she was a little girl, she had received special tutoring from the bookkeeper of a local grocery store. When she multiplied and divided, she slid the chestnut wood beads so rapidly on the bamboo rods that I worried about sparks starting to fly. Wang Tian enthusiastically tried to impart her skill to me, but to her great disappointment I showed no interest at all. My abacus was usually used to support my rear end as I rolled around the classroom. Quite often, before I could finish an equation, one of the beads, loosened by my roller skating, popped off and escaped to parts unknown.

Because of the ambitious literacy campaign launched by the new government, most of the primary schools had two shifts, one in the morning and one in the afternoon. Wang Tian and I were in the afternoon class.

Every day after lunch, Wang Tian came to our attic, and we walked to school together. Sometimes in the summer she came early. If I was still in the bathtub, she sat off to one side and chatted with my mother.

I no longer slept with Mother, but I still nagged her to wash me in my bath. I usually spent the whole morning running around, getting sweaty and dusty. Mother always forced me to bathe and change into clean clothes before going to school.

Since I took the bath for Mom's sake, she had to share in the work. Mother prepared the water for me; Mother undressed me; Mother soaped me and rinsed me. My responsibility was to lie in the tub and flip around at her request. Finally, it was Mother's duty to wipe me dry and dress me.

"Watch out," Father grumbled whenever he saw this ritual. "A spoiled cat will jump on the kitchen table."

Father, your warning has been proven legitimate. Many years later, this spoiled brat did something much worse than any spoiled cat could ever do.

Despite Father's complaints I continued to enjoy my bathing privileges. One day while Mother was soaping me, a pot on the stove boiled over. Mother passed the soap to Wang Tian and asked her to continue the job.

Standing in the middle of the tub, I turned my back to Wang Tian, allowing her to lather me up. First she worked on my neck, my shoulders, and my buttocks. Then she slid her hand between my legs to soap that awful place. I felt a tickling, mixed with another strange feeling. I squeezed my legs together, trying in vain to resist the invasion.

After soaping my back, Wang Tian asked me to turn around and face her. I pretended not to hear anything. She held my shoulders and tried to rotate me. I resisted silently. Wang Tian grabbed the soap and moved around to my front. I was startled! Covering my troublesome crotch with both hands, I crouched abruptly, splashing water all over Wang Tian's face. She was startled, too, and asked me what was wrong. I didn't answer. Instead, I turned to Mother for help.

"Mom, my stomach hurts."

Mother glanced at me.

"It's okay." With a smile on her face, she told Wang Tian, "He'll be fine in a minute."

Mom was right. In a minute I was fine. I stood up obediently and let Wang Tian continue washing me.

I felt her fingers circling on my skin. It was different from my mother's caress. Caressed by Mother, I felt as if I was floating in a giant ball of cloud. I was touched from all directions or I wasn't touched at all. I felt everything or I didn't feel anything. Maybe it was safety, maybe it was relaxation, maybe it was comfort, or maybe it was all of these mixed together, churned into an extremely sophisticated compound, leaving me with no way to distinguish the ingredients. I took it for granted. I didn't analyze it, and I didn't even think about it.

But when Wang Tian touched my skin, the feeling was sharp. I could clearly sense the trembling of each nerve end as it was triggered. I intercepted and tracked the location, force, speed, and direction of her invading fingers, although not for defense at all.

In Mother's arms my behavior was unbridled, naked, without any disguise. In Wang Tian's hands, however, I sneakily learned the skills of camouflage and self-control.

Standing in the bathtub, my head was rotated under Wang Tian's arms, left, right, zooming in and zooming out. I pretended nonchalance, humming an improvised tune. But my eyelids shuttered rapidly, snapping a series of pictures of the dark secrets hidden in the shadows under her arms.

Sometimes my head was pulled too close, closer than the minimum focal length of my eyes. No matter how hard I tried to focus, the subject at the root of her arms remained blurred. So I decided to close my eyes, feigning exhaustion from the mangling. But in truth, I merely switched to another sense. I sniffed the air, trying to catch every molecule of the scent wafting from her short sleeves.

The smell was strange. A little salty, a little sweet, sort of like overfermented rice wine with, perhaps, a baby's diaper among the rags that wrapped the fermentation barrel. It made me dizzy. I felt as if I had gulped down an entire bowl of warm sake. My fingers convulsed, but I held the contraction, letting the stress in the tendons spread and dissolve into a flood of goose bumps on my arms. Quietly they rose and quietly they faded. Nobody noticed.

I knew I had grown up.

CHAPTER FOUR

The Penglai Market

Every day, going to school, hand in hand, Wang Tian and I passed through the Penglai market.

Every day, returning from school, hand in hand, Wang Tian and I passed through the Penglai market.

The Penglai market was a ruin.

Some people said it had been hit by Japanese bombs during the war; others said there had been a fire ignited by an opium lamp. In any case, the Wonderland, once a fancy department store, was now nothing but a cracked expanse of crimson mosaic floor that fragmentarily flashed back to the luxuries of times gone by.

But no weeds were ever able to grow through the cracks. Instead, a splendid bouquet of popular entertainment sprouted there, which, along with the country's economy, flourished for a brief period after the revolution.

Many musical troupes, in styles ranging from northern Peking opera to southern Guangdong folk singing and accompanied by a vast variety of instruments, performed simultaneously in their distinctive dialects. Circles drawn on the ground in white chalk powder marked the neighboring stages. Standing between the circles, your left ear would be pounded by the basso profundo of a black-faced warrior bragging about his merits and successes, while your right ear was drilled by the piercing soprano of a white-lipped ghost seeking revenge for her lover's betrayal.

The vendors' performances were equally dramatic.

The tiger-bone tonic wine seller beat his rugged chest so hard that I wondered if the bones soaking in his big jar really came from a large cat or had just been shaken out of his rib cage.

The mute rat poison vendor silently watched people passing by. He advertised his merchandise with cold evidence: a heap of rats' tails lay at his feet.

The face of the popcorn vendor was dyed black by the smoke from his coal stove. With one hand he pumped the bellows; with the other he turned the bomb-shaped, cast-iron cooking drum. Every ten minutes or so, when the pressure in the drum built up to the bursting point, he yelled:

"H-e-ere it comes!"

Then he flung the lid open. A deafening bang! Like the eruption of a volcano, a cloud of popcorn exploded into his filthy basket.

In those years quite a few Russian refugees were still left in Shanghai. Former aristocrats, they had escaped from the Soviet Revolution to China (an odd decision) and bred second or even third generations in a foreign land. But they still had problems blending into the strictly homogenous Chinese society. Most of them were reduced to selling cheap wares like matches, spools of thread, or, most frequently, soap. They would beat their hairy hands on wooden crates and monotonously shout:

"Soap, soap!"

Their strange accent impaired effective verbal advertising, but their fair skin and transparent, greenish pupils subliminally hinted at the bleaching power of their merchandise.

Sometimes we saw Indians. The Sikhs had been brought to Shanghai by the British during colonial times, primarily to serve as gate watchmen. After the revolution their quiet personalities carried over into their new, meager businesses. Off in a corner of the market, a tall gloomy Indian crouched beside the hind legs of his horse. A huge, white turban rode above a pair of deeply socketed eyes. Patiently he waited for a rare customer to come over for a cup of freshly squeezed mare's milk. As a ritual, some mothers liked to feed their newborns a few spoonfuls of horse's milk. They believed that the galloping speed of the horse could boost the quickness of their babies' minds.

The cough remedy seller, perched on a tall stool, attracted clients by telling folk legends. Although I never bought a single cough drop, I was one of his biggest fans. I could stand for hours, craning to watch his flapping lips as he sprayed spittle that sparkled in the sun. Each time he paused his never-ending tale at a cliff-hanging moment to hawk his candies, I waited. I waited for the flying sword hanging frozen in midair to be defrosted. I waited for the knight halted at the beauty's bedroom door to be reanimated. I listened patiently to the merchant's chronic cough while he extolled the miraculous effect of his lozenges.

And the food!

Sticky-rice balls, fried rice cakes, scallion pancakes, steamed bread, meat-filled buns, boiled sesame dumplings, deep-fried pork steaks, skewers of barbecued lamb . . . Fragrant steam and greasy smoke rose and lingered above the Penglai market from dawn until midnight.

The panfried dumpling seller beat his flat pan with clanging energy. The poor dumplings scattered to the edges, as if debating whether leaping over the rim to their deaths would be preferable to enduring the heat and vibration any longer.

The steamed rice vendor, understanding that his wooden barrel could not survive the same rough treatment as his neighbor's steel pan, enthusiastically rattled his chopsticks in a bamboo cup to attract customers. I believed that this method also provided a low-tech "dry wash" for those dirty chopsticks.

And soups, there were all kinds of oily soups: cow's tripe soup, pig's bowel soup, lamb's lung soup, duck's blood soup . . . You had to be careful when you put your lips to the rim of the bowl. The oil floating on the soup was so thick that it entirely sealed in the steam. The soup looked cool, but it was hot, boiling hot.

One day, as usual, Wang Tian held my hand as we walked through the market. To my surprise, she leaned over and asked me, "Do you want some panfried buns?"

What a stupid question!

Four panfried buns cost five cents. If a customer bought eight of them he got a free bowl of egg-drop soup. Wang Tian paid ten cents.

The raw buns had just been put into the pan but I was already impatient. Grabbing our plate, I stood beside the stove.

Panfried buns are first fried in oil until half-browned. Then a sprinkling of water is added, and they are covered and steamed until done. They come out crisp on the bottom and tender on the top. And inside, a nugget of chopped meat soaking in hot juice!

The fragrance of oil and scallions escaped from the wooden lid along with the steam. It wafted into my nose and condensed into a mouthful of saliva. Suddenly the wooden lid was whisked away and a huge cloud of steam mushroomed upward. Before I could see a thing, two rows of sizzling hot buns had been plopped onto our plate.

I put the plate on a table and knelt on the bench. Frenziedly I blew on the buns to cool them.

"Nine," Wang Tian murmured.

"What did you say?" I asked.

"He goofed," she whispered. "He gave us an extra one."

"Lucky day!" I grabbed the vinegar bottle, ready to season the buns.

"Hold it," Wang Tian said. She picked up the plate and walked back to the stove. The vendor was beating his pan like crazy and I couldn't hear what Wang Tian said to him. All I saw was the guy picking a bun off our plate and tossing it back into the pan. The bun took an unexpected bounce, leapt out of the pan, and splashed down in the ditch!

"Idiot!" I pounded on the table, rattling the vinegar bottle.

Carrying the plate, Wang Tian returned to the table. She sat beside me and we shared the bowl of egg-drop soup and our eight buns.

I remember that I ate six.

CHAPTER FIVE

The Temple of Letters

Less than five minutes' walk north from the Penglai market stood the Temple of Letters. Though the noise of the market could still vaguely be heard, the scenery around the temple was peaceful.

Mother said the Temple of Letters was built to commemorate a *zhuangyuan*. A *zhuangyuan*? What's that? Mother said it was the title given to the scholar who took first place in the highest imperial writing examination. The emperor was extremely fond of this particular *zhuangyuan* and was prepared to reward him by offering his daughter's hand. Unfortunately the young scholar studied too hard and died spitting blood.

"Don't worry, my son," Mother paused in her story and added a footnote to comfort me. "You are far from spitting blood."

After he died, the *zhuangyuan* ascended into heaven and became the star of letters. On a summer evening, while sitting on the roof and enjoying the breeze, Mother pointed out that particular spot of light. Since you are going to be a scholar, Mother said, this is something you should know. Long gone is my memory of the star's location, but I still remember that it was red.

Along the walls of the Temple of Letters spread the vendors of comic books. The shelves that exhibited the books were well designed. Two racks hinged together as a pair were opened in the morning, closed in the evening. In front of the bookshelves were several benches. Their short legs and rough planks reminded me of crocodiles.

In the evening, when the vendors closed down their stalls, the benches were piled up and chained to a gnarled tree. Seen from a distance, they looked like bony horses tethered in the dusk.

The height for displaying a particular kind of comic book depended on the height of a particular age-group of readers. The highest level of the shelves held historical stories, legends of knights, science fantasy, and so on. I remember that I could hardly reach them even on tiptoe. The lowest level was for stories like *The Tortoise and the Hare, The Bear Brothers,* and *Mushroom Beauties.* Readers with dripping noses could lie comfortably on the ground and make their choices.

To read a newly released book cost one cent; old ones were two for a penny. The atmosphere around the vendors was pretty democratic—most of the legal readers sitting on the benches were willing to share the pages with the parasitic "lice."

"Lice" was the title given by the owner of the stall to those who read without paying. Sticking to the backs of the legal readers, a few heads on the left shoulder, a few on the right, plus a few heads above the paying head, they and their host formed a harmonious symbiotic system.

Though "lice" could not afford the one-penny rent, they were willing to perform some chore as a contribution. For example, fetching a popsicle for the host, stretching out a hand to shade the pages from the sun, or gently waving a palm-leaf fan, sending a breeze to every member of the group.

But sometimes, when the story reached a crucial point, a group discussion spontaneously erupted. Good guy or bad guy? Killed or escaped? The magic dagger was launched from the master's mouth or from his nose? And so on and so forth. Numerous fingers reached for the book, simultaneously pointing, gesturing, and flipping pages. Finally the host would lose his temper and all the lice would be expelled.

But those humble parasites were good-natured. Their tiny nervous systems had not evolved enough to contain full-sized dignity (which often proves to be the major source of misfortune). They would circle around for a while and gradually cluster behind the back of their host again.

I was one of the lice.

Sometimes I extended my duties from the host reader to the owner of the stall, running to buy a pack of cigarettes or helping him stack the benches when the stall closed down. Because of my outstanding service I became a "legal" louse, enjoying privileges similar to those conferred by an assistantship at an American college.

Quite often when a mini-reader, clutching a penny, did not know what book to pick, the owner snapped his fingers and hollered, "Hey you!" He was summoning me to offer help. I, of course, was more than happy to do that. I would choose a book on behalf of my host, but according to my height. And then I reversed the host-and-louse hierarchy—I sat and let the little one stand behind me as my parasite. But I wouldn't let the exploitation go too far. I explained one page after another, choosing the simplest words from my simple vocabulary. The little one nodded his head constantly, thinking he got every penny's worth out of his single penny.

I seldom saw any girls patronizing those stalls. Was it because girls had less tolerance for the swarms of parasites? Or simply because girls were smarter than boys, and they knew comic books were stupid?

The Temple of Letters was where my brothers and I frequently went to play. One day I dug out a cluster of tiny white eggs from the edge of the pond. I was excited and showed the eggs to my two brothers. Bao said that they were probably snake's eggs. Ling was scared and said to throw them away. I was scared, too, but didn't want to give them up.

Walking toward home, I carried them in my cupped palms. It was hot that day. The sun reflected off the eggs, searing my eyes. I heard a "crack" from between my hands, and a creature crawled out of a shell! I almost threw all the eggs to the ground, but I restrained myself. It was a turtle! As small as a button, but it had everything: head, back, claws, and a wiggling eyelash of a tail.

I ran home, put all the eggs in a bowl, and placed them in the sunshine on the roof. After a while, five miniature turtles cracked out of their shells one by one.

The baby turtles stayed with my family for only one night.

The next morning Mother escorted me as I brought the newborns back to the Temple of Letters and released all of them into the pond. Mother said that the pond was for believers who demonstrated their devotion by freeing captive animals such as fish, frogs, and turtles.

"Even though you boys are in a new school," Mother said, "it is best not to offend the old god of letters."

All the doors and windows of the temple were nailed shut. At that time, having too many crucial things to worry about, the new government had not yet tightened up its religious policy. The boarding up of the halls was probably done for safety reasons—the buildings were rotten. In early spring, the disintegrating tiles slid along with the melting snow and clattered down off the roof. The line of debris surrounding the hall served as a warning to potential trespassers.

At the south end of the Temple of Letters stood a seven-story pagoda in which the statue of the *zhuangyuan* was worshipped. One summer evening after school let out, it was still fairly light. When we passed the Temple of Letters, I asked Wang Tian:

"Do you want to climb up to the top of the pagoda?"

Before Wang Tian could make up her mind, I had already dragged her to the bottom of the tower.

The pagoda was shut, just like the halls in the temple, but I knew a secret passage. I pulled up a few boards, asking Wang Tian to stick her head through. But she stepped back.

"Fine. But I'm going anyway." I slithered into the hole.

"Wait, wait!" Wang Tian's head peeked into the hole. I knew it. I pulled her through. Side by side we stood in the pagoda. It was dark. A shaft of sunlight knifed through a crack in a wooden panel, slashing across the face of the statue. It lit up a dusty eyeball. A few bats were startled. Dust curled upward in the beam of light. The god's eye was smoking.

Wang Tian grabbed my hand.

"Let's get out of here, okay?" she whispered.

"Since we're already in here," I said, "we'd be chicken not to climb up."

I started to climb the stairs. Steps squeaked under my feet.

"Wait, wait," Wang Tian said. "I think I should go first."

That was fine by me. So with Wang Tian above me, we spiraled our way up. Wang Tian was wearing a skirt that day. Every time she passed through the beam of sunshine, I saw her legs. One flash at each level. During the first couple of circles I missed the scene, but as we rose higher I decided on a sneak attack. I lifted my head, holding my breath. Here came the flash! Yes, I saw it. In a split second I caught sight of her calves, her legs. The last flash, however, gave me a shock—a line of blood shone on the inside of her left thigh.

"Hold on," I stopped her. "You've scratched your leg!"

She halted. In the dim light leaking in through the top panel, I saw her reach a hand into the folds of her skirt. She sat down on the step and put a handkerchief under the fabric.

"It's okay," she said.

"It is not okay! It is not . . ."

"Shut up, will you?" She smiled.

On the way back I noticed Wang Tian walked slowly.

That night, I bragged about my adventure in the pagoda to my mother and casually mentioned Wang Tian's scratch.

"Where?" Mother asked.

"Here," I pointed at the inside of my legs and said, "She was bleeding here."

Mother smiled. Yet the smile froze. Mother was scared.

"I knew it wasn't okay. Do you think she's all right," I asked.

"Yes."

"Then what are you scared of, Mom?"

"That place," Mother did not look at me, "the pagoda, women are not supposed to climb those stairs."

About a month later, a thunderstorm was pending. I sat at the window, watching the clouds. Without the warning of a flash, a deafening thunderclap abruptly boomed. I was startled and fell on the floor, crushing an aluminum pan.

The pagoda was hit by lightning. One of the upturned eaves of the roof was blasted into rubble. It created a sensation in our neighborhood. Some people said that it had happened because a giant evil snake resided in the pagoda. Others suggested that, during the Chin dynasty, a cold-blooded robber had hidden his cursed treasure in the belly of the statue, and for two hundred years the *zhuangyuan* had remained silent. Finally divine retribution for his acceptance of bribes had arrived. Yet another theory claimed that during the thunderstorm a spy had hidden himself on the top floor of the tower. He had stuck out an antenna, sending radio information to Taiwan.

The last hypothesis sounded the most scientific and the most politically correct.

At the beginning of the fourth grade, Wang Tian dropped out of school. She married. Her husband was a traffic policeman.

A couple of years later, when I had already entered junior high, Wang Tian came to the attic for the last time. I was not at

home. Mother told me that Wang Tian had come to say good-
bye to us. She and her husband were going back to their hometown in Anhui Province, and her mother was going with them.

Wang Tian's husband had come to Shanghai before the revolution and had been a police officer under the former regime.
After the revolution, he was allowed to work for the new government. But when the new police force was established, he,
along with his family, was asked to leave the city and go back to
his remote village.

Ever since then I have not heard from Wang Tian.

In the decades that have passed since Wang Tian descended
from our attic, much has happened in Anhui: floods, drought,
insect plagues, and other, not-to-be-mentioned, disasters. In the
early 1960s, 43 million Chinese died of hunger, and Anhui
Province suffered the heaviest toll.

Every time I saw refugees curled up on the sidewalk, begging
with the accents of Anhui, I hoped I would find Wang Tian.
And almost immediately I would be scared by my imagination.

Good luck, Wang Tian and your family.

CHAPTER SIX

Anecdotes About the Roof

A three-story building occupied numbers 476 through 486 on Penglai Road. My family lived in the attic at number 480. The attic possessed the only window that opened out onto the roof of the building. That seventy feet or so of roof became our exclusive colony, generously compensating us for the cramped continent inside.

In the early 1950s there were few high buildings around Penglai Road, so the roof of our attic was the high ground of the neighborhood. Looking north from the roof, we could see the gray silhouettes of the International Hotel, the First Department Store, and the Shanghai Mansion all squatting on the horizon. To the south, the smokestacks of the ships in the Huangpu River glided silently on a black sea of fish-scale tiled roofs.

The attic roof was the perfect place for our family to air its bedding.

Shanghai faces the sea and, even in winter, the humidity is high. Bedding left unaired for a few weeks becomes cold and damp. Each night, the first touch of the comforter raises goose bumps all over your body.

So early on the weekends, if the sky was clear, all the neighborhood families divided up the sidewalks. Before the sun had even risen, the long benches that occupied the sidewalks were labeled with the families' names. Then the sun peeped through the gaps between the buildings, hastily scanned the assorted bedding spread on the benches, and moved on to hang out somewhere else.

Sometimes a cigarette butt was flung from a passing pedicab and burned a large hole in one of the comforters. That was just bad luck; nobody could be blamed.

My family was privileged. We didn't have to get up early. The sun had the whole morning to dry the dew or frost on the roof thoroughly. By noon the roof tiles were warm, and we would then carry all the straw pallets, pillows, comforters, and sheets out through the window and spread them on the roof. Just like in an oven, they were baked from both sides. We did not have to take them in until the sun reddened in the west. At night, after we turned off the light, the whole attic was permeated by the smell of the sun.

In winter, if there was a big snowfall, we had an inexhaustible source of pure water. Climb out the window, scoop up a potful of snow, and we had plenty for cooking and tea. In such a crowded city, the exclusive enjoyment of so much pristine snow was an extravagant luxury.

Occasionally, if the wind changed direction, the chimney of

the hot water shop in the next block cast a sprinkling of dark ashes on the snow. This, however, was still much better than the pungent odor of chlorine and sewage that flavored the city's tap water. The six members of our family could not consume all the heavenly water from the roof, and we were happy to share our bounty with our neighbors. Snows came and snows went. In the thirty years we lived in the attic, few ever came to enjoy them with us. The soiled background of our family, I believed, must have polluted the white snow. Alas!

In summer, the breezes that blessed the roof were another great pleasure. When the sun set, we splashed water onto the tiles to dispel the residual heat and the whole family gathered on the roof to enjoy the unfettered breezes.

To climb onto the roof, we had to be barefoot. That was a rule set by Father and Mother. Breaking a few roof tiles was not a minor problem, but slippery shoesoles held the greater danger. Extra security measures were imposed on two members of our family—my sister and me. My two brothers had freedom, more or less, but Chuen and I were clamped between my parents. Any commotion would immediately put us in the crossfire of their eyes. Even worse, Father tied a finger-thick rope around each of our waists, leashing us like two dogs. Mother held Chuen's and Father held mine. My sister was still a little creature, but to me, a pupil in grammar school, this was really humiliating!

In fact, Father himself should have been more careful. He had once almost dropped a stove off the roof. He may have been too cocky, because almost nobody else had the privilege of starting a stove on such a peak.

Every morning millions of stoves, spewing dense smoke, were brought out to the sidewalks. Housewives fanned the stoves furiously, tearing and coughing. Without complaint, pedestrians dodged in and out of the clouds of smoke like veteran firefighters.

My family never used a fan to start its stove. We put our stove on the roof and stuffed a lighted newspaper inside. Then we only had to drop firewood and coal into the chamber. In seconds, the wind would excite the smoke into a burst of flame.

That day Father, for some reason, didn't position the stove securely. He had just put the newspaper into the chamber when the stove tumbled down along the slanted tiles. It seemed determined to smash a few of the heads moving over the sidewalk below. During the split second in which the stove rolled over the edge of the roof, its handle caught on the hook that held the gutter. Pedestrians gasped and screamed, watching thirty pounds of metal and clay dangling under the gutter and the burning newspaper gracefully dancing in the air. Thank goodness, Father had not yet packed the wood and coals into the chamber. Otherwise the volcanic eruption onto the pedestrians' heads would definitely have condemned him to hell.

When I got a little older, I liked to lie flat on the roof by myself, watching the sky before a thunderstorm. The low-altitude rain clouds, like black bombers in complex formation, flew over my head. Yet the white cumulonimbus, high above, remained motionless and emotionless, observing the air raid below.

I often counted the seconds between the lightning and the thunder, attempting to feel the immensity of the universe. Sometimes the lightning flashed so close by that I could not count at all before the thunder exploded. Maybe it was static electricity; maybe it was terror—all my hair stood on end. But I didn't move. The prickly numbness on my face gradually dispersed over my whole body. Excitement fused with trembling.

Suddenly my face was struck by a raindrop. It hurt. A series of single shots followed. Then a volley hit, leaving the roof tiles pocked with dark traces. Finally the storm began intense strafing. Steam rose from the roof like smoke.

Once a year the fireworks celebrating National Day created a breathtaking spectacle. On October 1, beginning in the afternoon, millions of people rushed to People's Square. By evening all of the streets surrounding the square were jammed. But our family, like aristocrats, avoided hobnobbing with the crowds. After dinner Mother made us put on our padded-cotton jackets and the whole family adjourned to the roof. We had snacks: sunflower seeds, pumpkin seeds, peanuts, and popped rice. We nibbled as we waited for the sky to grow dark.

Finally the first fireworks rose. No sound, only bright colors unfolding silently in the sky. We cheered in unison. Only after five or six seconds did the crackling reach us.

I remember a kind of firework that shot out a skyful of parachutes, each carrying a flare as it floated through the night. Sometimes the autumn north wind propelled them toward our home. One after another, they passed low over our heads. They drifted so close that I could see the strings of the parachutes.

Once a blue light, dangling beneath a parachute, descended right toward our roof. We four children screamed. Just as the ball of light drifted overhead, I reached out to catch it. My fingers were singed, but the parachute continued its southward flight, passing one roof after another, landing nowhere. We were very disappointed. Then everyone gathered to look at my fingers and smell them one by one, trying to comprehend the mystery of the flare through the dark ash on my fingertips.

During my first year of middle school, I constructed a homemade telescope. Although my telescope had only two lenses, its magical power mesmerized me. How could it grab distant objects and yank them right up to my nose?

I tested my instrument on the roof. First I looked south. There was a fire-watching tower there, very tall, standing on the horizon, showing only as a blackish silhouette. I focused my telescope on it. I caught sight of a window at the top of the tower. There was a head in the window. I stared at it. It was a man, holding binoculars, gazing in my direction. I waved at him, and that man waved back at me! I squealed with joy. But the man had no more time to spend with me. I was disappointed when he turned to look in another direction.

Then I turned my lens to the building across the street. It was about thirty yards away, but I could see a cat squatting on the edge of the roof, its whiskers glittering in the sunshine. I scanned downward, focusing on a window. The curtain was half-open. As I was about to turn my lens away, my eyes were transfixed—a back, a woman's white back, with pink bra marks! The woman passed behind the curtain. She reappeared and vanished again. I held my breath and attempted to stabilize the shaking of the tube. I waited, trying to catch the target once more. How long did I wait? I couldn't tell. Maybe only a few seconds, maybe a few hours. A truck honked in the street below. I jumped. I put down my telescope, rubbing my blurry eyes. When I collected my nerves enough to look through the lens again, the curtain had been closed.

When my brother Ling was young, he was addicted to crickets. He had a delicate temperament, with great reserves of patience, and he served his crickets like a slave. Though my big brother, Bao, and I were far from experts, we could tell at a glance that Ling's treasures were dross. With tiny heads and thin legs, they chirped heroically all night in their own pots. But when we put one of Ling's loud warriors in the fighting pot, the sight of the enemy would literally scare the shit out of him—as he escaped, he dropped a disgusting trail along the floor of the arena.

But Ling did not mind our sneers and laughter. Every day he cleaned scores of cricket pots, gave his pets food, and changed their water. When the weather got hot, he drove the crickets into the water for a refreshing bath. After their ablutions, Ling prodded their mandibles with a grass poker. This procedure made them vibrate their wings and chirp themselves dry, preventing the onset of insect arthritis. The problem was that Ling was too delicate and too slow. By the time he had served his scores of masters, the sun was setting and his homework still lay undone. So Mother became determined to intervene.

One day Ling returned home after school. As usual, he dropped his schoolbag and went to greet his masters. To his surprise, the soapbox that held the cricket pots was in chaos—Mother had thrown all of his crickets out the window onto the roof. Ling jumped up the ladder and looked out the window. There were millions of gaps between the overlapping tiles. Where should he start to search?

That evening crickets called in chorus from all parts of the roof. Ling wept late into the night.

From that day on crickets dwelt and bred in the safe haven of our roof. The gaps between the tiles made wonderful nests, and abundant moss and dewdrops provided inexhaustible food and drink. Each year, from early fall until the beginning of winter, crickets called every night. For thirty years they accompanied our family through the cold and the heat, the bitter and the sweet.

CHAPTER SEVEN

Going to the Great World

For the first three or four years after we moved to Shanghai, going to the Great World was the once-a-year grand event for my family.

At that time my father was working in a plastic button factory housed on the street level of the building in which we lived. Father's job was to drive the flywheel.

Plastic buttons were formed by molding plastic powder with heat and pressure. The lower part of the button press contained a charcoal stove for heating the steel mold. The upper part of the press was a giant cast-iron flywheel, roughly four feet in diameter with handles all around. There was no motor to drive the hefty flywheel; the power came from my father.

Being a flywheel driver was a majestic and impressive occupation. The mold operator first put the plastic powder into the mold; he then hit a small bell, "Ding!"—the signal to apply pressure. Grabbing the shiny steel handles, with a roar Father

37

spun the flywheel. Under the explosive force generated by the muscles of his arms, back, and waist, the flying wheel whirled downward. The handles blurred into a silver halo. "Bang!" the flywheel hit the mold. After two minutes of heat, the powder pressed in the mold solidified into glossy buttons.

The workshop was hot. Even in winter Father went bare-chested. His silhouette was projected against the wall and ceiling by the orange flames in the stove. His sweaty muscles gleamed against his gigantic, dashing shadows.

That was the strongest Father ever looked in my memory.

The year the Communist Party took over Shanghai, Father was about fifty. His salary was sixty Chinese dollars per month. Rice cost eight cents per pound; pork, sixty cents per pound. The next three or four years were a period of great prosperity for my family. After survival came entertainment.

The Great World was a four-story entertainment complex built in the 1930s by the head of the powerful local "Blue Blood" mob. For twenty years before and ten years after the revolution, every afternoon, from two o'clock to ten o'clock, the Great World provided a variety of popular entertainment for thousands of ordinary people. Admission was inexpensive—adults paid fifteen cents each; children, ten cents. You could not get a ticket unless you arrived early and stood in a long line.

The box office didn't open until one o'clock, but my family started marching toward the Great World as early as eight in the morning.

We prepared carefully for the trip. A few days before the outing, Mother washed and starched a set of clothes for each member of the family. She folded these "visiting suits" and put them into a trunk, to await the grand occasion.

We always went to the Great World on a Sunday, so on Saturday, after work, Father took his three sons to have their hair cut. There was a barbershop right next door to our house. A row of chrome-plated barber chairs stood on the white, tiled floor. Mirrors glared from every direction. But all that luxury had nothing to do with us.

Why should hair be cut in the barber's shop? Father eloquently queried. No matter how soft your chairs, no matter how crisp your mirrors, I can't eat them.

So leading his subordinates past the barber's neon lights, Father marched us toward the street vendor of haircuts, who fit perfectly into the socioeconomic status of our family.

The haircut vendor was located under the east wall of the Temple of Letters. One rickety cane chair. Three bamboo rods forking around a chipped enamel basin. Under the basin hung a grimy towel. Although the fungus growing on the mirror blurred your face, the setting sun reflected in the peeling silver coating still dazzled your eyes.

Because we were regular customers of the vendor and patronized him as a group, we always enjoyed the wholesale price— children cost eight cents each; adults, ten. It cost two cents more to have your head washed. But my brothers and I never cost our father those two extra cents.

Why should kids have their heads washed by the vendor? Again Father's reasoning was convincing: You can buy a bottle of hot water for one cent and wash three heads and still have enough for a cup of tea! Father himself, however, never saved those two cents. He always had his head shaved. Even if Father's scalp could stand "dry" shaving, the barber's Swiss razor wouldn't survive the torture.

The food for the trip, panfried wheat flour, was prepared on Saturday evening.

Early Sunday morning we got up eagerly. The attic was in a tumult. Mother took the "visiting suits" from the trunk and let everybody dress. Made of heavy-duty, coarse cotton cloth and starched with left-over water from boiled rice, those suits felt like bullet-proof armor, rattling whenever our limbs moved.

Father had to report to the local police station three days before the trip and request permission for our outing. Although he had abandoned all his property and moved thousands of miles from his homeland, he was still labeled as a landlord and had been sentenced to three years of public surveillance. Public surveillance was not a big deal, Father thought. It meant nothing but being under everybody's noses, being sniffed and watched all the time. Once a year, he applied for a fun trip to Great World with his family, and his application was always granted.

"Behave yourself!" Police Officer Chang, who was in charge of security in our neighborhood, always added a warning to his approval.

"Yes, yes, behave myself, behave . . ." Father always bowed again and again as he stepped backward.

Only once in my memory was our trip postponed for a week. That particular Sunday, the foreign affairs minister of the Soviet Union visited Shanghai. Father, Mother, and my brother Bao were ordered to stay home all day. Bao was twelve years old.

I remember when we first visited the Great World, Mother was still breast-feeding my sister, Chuen. Tormented early in the morning by a commotion she could not make head or tail of, my little sister fell back to sleep on the way to the Great World. Her small head lolled around while her little rear end ballooned the baby sling.

My sister strapped on her back, Mother carried a heavy basket covered by a white towel. Under the towel were bowls, chopsticks, spoons, cups, and so on. Chuen's spare diapers were stuffed between the china.

Father was fully laden, too. In his left hand, he carried a one-gallon tin in which the panfried wheat flour was tightly packed. From his right hand dangled two one-gallon thermos bottles filled with hot water. Hot water was available in the Great World, a cup for one penny.

"Highway robbery!" Father said.

By nine o'clock the line in front of the box office extended around behind the Great World and on into Yunnan Road. We sat on the sidewalk surrounded by our supplies and gear. Father, leaning against the wall, stretched out his legs and started a comfortable nap. Mother sat on the curb and untied my sister from her back. She put the baby face down on her lap and changed her diaper. Then Mother unbuttoned her blouse. Amid the turbulent waves of city noise, Mother peacefully fed her daughter.

Yunnan Road was a galaxy of fancy restaurants: Sichuan Restaurant, Hunan Restaurant, Wuxi Restaurant, Guangdong Restaurant . . . The doors swung constantly, fanning the greasy steam outside to linger on the sidewalk.

It was lunchtime.

Mother took the bowls out of the basket and Father pried open the tin. On the sidewalk we set up our picnic feast. Mother scooped the panfried wheat flour into bowls, then poured in hot water. She stirred with chopsticks. Each of us got a bowl of steaming flour paste.

"Mmm, it's sweet!" we cheered.

We had not known that Father would add sugar to the wheat flour. The hint of a smile flickered on Father's face.

We slurped joyfully.

Mother fed my sister with a tiny spoon while keeping an eye on the passersby, making sure no one kicked over the thermos bottles. People often stopped and watched us, but we did not care. We attended to our own business of eating. We ate, ate with contentment, ate with grace and clear consciences.

CHAPTER EIGHT

Taxi Hopping

In the early 1950s, if you were browsing in the Penglai market and spent ten cents or so for a dish of panfried meat-filled buns, the experience would certainly be unforgettable.

With the first bite, a geyser of hot meat juices unexpectedly shot from the corner of your lips and burned a hole in the tire of a pedicab parked across the street. While the customers gasped in admiration of your extraordinary performance, I hope you took a moment to remember the unseen contribution of my mother and her three boys.

Every morning around ten o'clock, carrying a bamboo basket covered with a white towel, Mother walked toward the Penglai market. She reached the back of the panfried bun stall.

"Here are the goods," she whispered to the owner.

"How many pounds?" the owner asked, a cigarette flapping between his lips.

"Same as yesterday," Mother said.

"Okay."

Her body blocking the sight of the diners sitting on the benches, Mother lifted the towel and dumped the goods from the basket into a jar. She closed the lid of the jar, accepted the money from the owner, and quietly left.

The goods were pork skin.

The filling for the buns is made of two parts of lean pork, and one part of pork fat. What makes the filling extremely juicy is another one part of pork skin. The fresh skin must be boiled overnight and run through a meat grinder. For all its humble appearance, the skin, in fact, has a high protein content. At room temperature, the protein gelatin from the skin holds the filling together. Cooking melts the modest ingredient into a mouthful of delicious juice.

Perhaps because of the unpleasant image of the skin or out of a concern for the confidentiality of their recipe, the owners of the stalls usually preferred secret delivery of the special ingredient.

Pork skin was the by-product of making pork grease, Mother's first business in Shanghai. The raw material from which the grease was extracted was pork fat. My brothers and I were the pork fat buyers.

Almost every morning at half-past five Mother dragged her sons out of bed. A few minutes later, three yawning boys walked down a gravel road darkened by heavy dew. Heading toward our assigned markets, we each carried a basket. The markets did not open until seven, but we had to reach them much earlier to line up or the fat would all be gone.

My sister, Chuen, was too young to share the responsibility

of earning our livelihood then. But she later made a much heavier sacrifice for our common survival.

As an incentive for our hard work, Mother gave each of us a five-cent piece to spend on our journey. Two cents for a roasted sesame pancake, three cents for fried dough. Wrapping the pancake around the dough, we held the food with both hands. We ate as we walked. Our palms were warmed, though the back of our hands were still chilly.

The market designated as mine was the farthest, but I was always the first to arrive back home. I had a trick.

When I finished shopping, I picked up the basket, now heavily loaded with fat, and staggered my way out of the market. The market was starting its rush hour. By the time I managed to reach the intersection, I was pooped. I put down my load and sat on the curb to take a break.

I was nine years old, and the muscles in my arms were far less voluptuous than the fat in the basket. Mother had wrapped layers of rags around the basket handle, but the weight of the cursed pig still cut into the thin tendons in the crook of my elbow. My arm was sore and numb.

Why not "taxi hop"?

Taxi hopping was a game I played when I was around seven or eight and a little bit mischievous. At that time almost everybody had seen a movie entitled *Railroad Guerrilla*. Those guerrillas stole Japanese military supplies, hopping with great ease on and off trains hurtling at full speed. They were our heroes and we emulated them. Of course, there were no locomotives running through the city's narrow streets. So the unfortunate taxi tricycles became our substitute targets.

On the back of every pedicab was a bumper, which was the perfect riding spot for stowaways. We kids appeared to be idly hanging about on the street corner, yet our eyes followed every taxi tricycle intently. As soon as the chosen cab dashed by, a kid leaped on the bumper and grabbed the back edge of the cabin.

Getting on board the taxi, however, did not necessarily mean success. Quite often the raider was discovered immediately. The pedaller would look over his shoulder and roar. The intruder, tumbled down off the bumper, would rub his scraped knees and ignore the laughter of his peers.

Locomotives are driven by steam; tricycles are propelled by muscles. Although a boy may not be especially heavy, adding some fifty pounds to a pair of calves already gnarled with veins is a big imposition. It took all the expertise of a master to add one's weight to a taxi and not be noticed.

I was one of the masters.

Describing my feat with the mechanical terminology I learned later, I attribute my consistent success to "the gradual increase of load."

First I ran. Following the pedicab, barefoot, I ran as quietly as a cat. Then I reached out my left hand and caught the edge of the cabin. I bent down and grabbed the bumper with my right hand. Still running, I smoothly shifted my weight from my feet to my right arm, which remained clamped to the bumper.

The pedaller could probably sense the increased resistance, but many factors—the slope of the road, the hardness of the asphalt, the velocity of the wind—were involved in any change in resistance. Although my procedure could not eliminate my mass, the point was to reduce as much as possible the "shocking load" that exposed most of the also-rans.

The taxi passed two or three telephone poles before my center of gravity completely shifted to the bumper. It was time to board. My arms pulled my body into the air, only to land softly on the bumper. No jumping, no shock; every move was gradual and smooth. Then I raised my left arm, signaling my success to my comrades.

Back then it had been a game, but now I set out to do business.

A pedicab was approaching the intersection. I still sat on the curb. I did not move my neck to scan the target; only my eyeballs tracked it. I held my breath, concentrating my energy. At the precise moment that the tricycle sped by, my leg muscles fired, launching me and my basket. I ran after the taxi, lugging the fat-packed basket. My legs struggled to provide the necessary speed while my arms suspended the weight in the air. Smoothly I loaded the basket onto the bumper. The situation had changed, but the principle remained—"the gradual increase of load."

Yes, I did it!

I ran on, following the bumper, free of load, full of joy.

As for whether I myself should board, the decision was based on my estimation of the potential power of the driver. If the pedaller was young and muscular, well, I would quite probably add on the extra weight. If the pedaller was old with wizened legs, I would never be too greedy. On the contrary, if the asphalt was sticky under the hot sun, I would bend over, pushing the bumper slightly when we traveled uphill.

I kept my secret from Mother, but I repeatedly introduced my two brothers to my skill, even presenting them with a couple of demonstrations. My brothers, however, consistently ignored my ingenuity and enthusiasm. More than a few times, when I flashed by on board my limousine and looked back at my brothers struggling with their fully laden baskets, I felt quite sorry for their hopeless conservatism.

CHAPTER NINE

Sizzling Grease

After we carried the pork home, Mother flensed the fat from the skin with a sharp knife. Then she diced the fat into small chunks, put them in a cast-iron cauldron, and fried them.

First the steam came out; then the hot scent of the grease. The fat gradually shrank in the cauldron, finally leaving only brownish cracklings floating in the sizzling grease. Mother removed the cracklings with a wire strainer, ladled the hot grease into a ceramic jar, and let it cool. The cracklings could be sold to a soybean milk vendor, who used them as a garnish. Sprinkled onto a bowl of hot soybean milk, the cracklings added flavor and crunch.

The pork grease, Mother's main product, was sold separately as an essential flavoring for noodle or wonton soup. This multi-faceted business went on for about two years until a catastrophe almost took my sister, Chuen, from us.

When Chuen was three years old, she still wore open-crotch pants that revealed two banana-shaped slices of her bottom. She liked to climb the wooden ladder that leaned against the south window. The slanted roof outside the window was a constant temptation to her. But she was only allowed to climb three steps, poke her head outside, and sneak a peek at the world. As soon as her little foot moved toward the fourth rung of the ladder, a slap on her bottom was guaranteed. In addition to the hygienic convenience, I presume this was another technical advantage of the classic open-crotch pants.

The second area forbidden to my sister was the trapdoor in the attic floor. Sometimes she stuck out her rear end in her strenuous efforts to lift the door. Quite a few times she came close to succeeding. Her exertions in trying to raise the heavy door caused her to lean precariously into the opening, giving us a real scare when we caught her. Our downstairs neighbor's cooking area was directly below our trapdoor. Often there was a pot of hot water bubbling on his stove. The steam penetrated up through our trapdoor into the attic. We dared not imagine the consequences of my sister's diving through the opening. We were aware of the boiling water under the door at all times, but we ignored the sizzling fat on our own stove.

One day I came home from school. As usual, I called from under the trapdoor:

"Open up!"

But there was no response. Something was dripping down through the crack in the door. I thought my sister had peed on the floor again. I lifted the door and felt something warm and slippery on my hand. I sniffed my fingers. Grease! I jumped up into the attic.

It was a mess.

The cauldron lay on the floor and grease was everywhere. A deformed, tiny, pink plastic slipper lay curled in a puddle, testifying to the temperature at the time of the accident. The coals in the stove were still glowing, but where were the people?

I could hardly find a dry spot to place my feet, but I managed to lift the cauldron and put it on the table. I grabbed a mop and swabbed the floor. When the mop was saturated with grease I wrung it into the cauldron. A pool of dirty grease soon accumulated in the bottom of the pot.

An elderly, bad-tempered man nicknamed "Old Ginger" lived downstairs. He would grab a broom and bang on his ceiling whenever a drop of water seeped down from the attic. Now the whole floor was soaked with grease. I was worrying, when I heard crying from below. I pulled up the slippery door. My brother, Ling, wept as he climbed up the steps. With every sob he hiccuped, but I managed to get the story out of him—Chuen had been burned by the oil.

I dashed downstairs and ran toward the hospital.

In the emergency room I saw my sister. What I really saw was a ball of gauze. Only two small, fluttering nostrils let me know my sister was still alive.

My whole family was there.

Mother was picking at the gauze as she cried, as if the neatness of the bandages was crucial to her daughter's survival. Father gazed at the dripping glucose bottle. His head nodded with every drop, or maybe the liquid dripped only when his head nodded.

Mother told me that Chuen had overturned the cauldron.

The gauze covered my sister's eyes, too. My heart was leaden.

I figured that in the future I would have to hold Chuen's hand and guide her along the street each day. But I didn't dare speak my fears.

The next morning I saw a bamboo cup of rice underneath the Bodhisattva's picture. Two red sticks protruded from the rice. The incense had been burned, leaving its ashes on the grains. Under the bamboo cup lay a folded slip of paper. I opened the paper. Drawn awkwardly on it were two eyes.

Mother shared my worries, but she had also kept silent.

Lady Bodhisattva, I know you are very kind, and you must know I like your toes. If you don't like me to like your toes, I won't like them anymore. If you like me to like them, then I will still like them. Anyway, Lady Bodhisattva, could you please save my little sister? Let her live, live with a pair of eyes? Lady Bodhisattva, you must know it is awful to be blind. One time a fly landed on one of your eyebrows. Holding the flyswatter in my hand, I hesitated, and that big fly escaped. Lady Bodhisattva, you must know I always cheat when we play hide-and-seek. I don't mean to cheat, but the darkness behind the blindfold really scares me. I know my sister will have many scars, but I don't care. Other people don't have to like her; I will like her. I will play with her all my life. Lady Bodhisattva . . .

Old Ginger did not bang on our floor. Instead, he bought a big grapefruit and came to the hospital. He said that grapefruit is cool and refreshing, and insisted that we let Chuen eat it. But nobody could figure out how to feed it to her through the gauze.

Later Old Ginger changed his ceiling paper time and time again, but traces of grease kept seeping through. Mice crawled on his ceiling and left droppings on his pillow every night.

Police Officer Chang came to the hospital, too. Solemnly, he bent to inspect the gauze bundle on the bed. Then he turned to my parents and said, "Be careful in the future."

"Yes, yes, be careful," Father said.

"Yes, yes, be careful," Mother said.

About ten days later, the doctor unwrapped the gauze from Chuen's eyes. Her eyes were still closed. Over and over again, the nurse soaked and wiped away the crusty ooze from Chuen's swollen eyelids. The eyelids quivered, then quivered again. Chuen's eyes opened!

My heart stopped.

Her pupils slowly spun. From Mother's face they turned to Father's face, then from Father's face to each of her three brothers, one by one.

Two sparkling tears rolled down her cheeks.

Mother cried. My brothers and I cried.

Lady Bodhisattva, I know you are very kind.

CHAPTER TEN

Pigs' Heads

Not long after my sister's accident, Mother closed down her pork grease enterprise. The timing suggests a connection between the accident and the closing of the business. As a writer, I wish there was—it could have provided a whole chapter of sophisticated psychological conflict for my book. Yet the facts were simple and concrete.

Even if my sister had died from her burns, as long as the fat business could continue to feed her three remaining kids, Mother would, without hesitation, have continued to fill the attic with the fumes of sizzling grease.

Consider the peasants who live around the volcanoes of Bali. Phosphorous smoke circles ominously around the top of the crater, day and night. Lava is obviously more terrifying than any grease. Yet the peasants, bending over in the rice paddies, plant seedlings, one row after another. The searing memories of the catastrophes that torched their ancestors to ashes are quietly buried in the cool mud.

The reason Mother stopped her grease business was simple: the newly formed, state-run grease company purchased all the pork fat in Shanghai.

Mother shifted her attention to pigs' heads.

My brothers and I became unemployed. One or two pigs' heads per day were more than sufficient for Mother's new business. She began selling cooked pigs' head meat.

Good-bye, my taxi hopping!

Pigs' heads are hairy. If you pulled out the hairs one by one with tweezers, you could work on a single chin until your own beard turned gray. So a new technique was employed. The stove remained the same, and so did the cauldron. But what sizzled inside was no longer grease; now it was rosin.

When the block of rosin had melted, Mother submerged the pig's head in the cauldron and stirred it around. Then she lifted up the head, now covered in a sheath of rosin, and dipped it in cold water. When she peeled the wax-like rosin off the skin, all the hairs came with it. The rosin could be reheated again and again, each time with the increasing stink of burnt hair.

Then came the good part—the cooking.

The head was boiled in "old soup." There were myriad seasonings in "old soup": ginger, garlic, sugar, vinegar, cinnamon, tea leaves, cooking wine, soy sauce, and so on. A cloud arose from the simmering pot so mouthwatering that even the knots in the beams overhead seemed to be steamed into shiny meatballs.

"Old soup"—the older the better. Every time it was used, a cup of water and a spoonful of salt were added. There was a shop on Yunnan Road that sold cooked rabbit meat. On its sign a gilded inscription proclaimed:

ONE-HUNDRED-YEAR-OLD SOUP

Unfortunately Mother's small pot of "old soup" lasted only three years. Then it was flushed away by the red wave of a deprivatization campaign.

Every day for three years Mother headed for her vendor's booth around four o'clock in the afternoon. She carried her heavy utensils and the cooked meat suspended from a shoulder pole. The bamboo rod, bowed under its burden, squeaked rhythmically along with Mother's bouncing tread. Every couple of blocks Mother switched the pole from one shoulder to the other, but she did not need to stop. She caught the bamboo pole at the height of its bounce and, with an elegant swing of her neck, dipped her head under it. The whole load was smoothly transferred to the other side.

The booth was set in front of a wineshop, about half a mile from home. There was a kind of symbiosis between the wineshop and the meat stall. A customer stepping out of the shop with a bottle of rice wine was assailed by the fragrance of the meat, which became all but irresistible. In the meat booth, the steam, circling above the red, glossy pig's head, subliminally suggested the pleasures of the warm wine. This mutually beneficial relationship led the wineshop owner to allow Mother not only a spot on his doorstep but also a place in his store for her heavy utensils during bad weather.

The Chinese have comprehensive tastes. Except for the bones and hair (which are still waiting to get onto a menu), all parts of a pig's head are considered delicacies. And they are cheap. Ears and tongues have a wonderful, elastic texture. The two eyeballs are not overlooked, either. Sprinkled with salt and wild pepper and wrapped in a dried lotus leaf, they can be popped into your mouth while your own eyes are fixed on a movie screen.

The pig's brain is even more tender than tofu. And it's therapeutic, too. For centuries Chinese physicians propounded the theory that what you eat strengthens the corresponding part of your body. Eating giblets, for example, enhances digestion; dining on kidneys improves urination; and consuming liver enriches the blood. Sometimes the functional correlation was more sophisticated and could only be understood symbolically. For example, rhinoceros horn won the honor of being the miraculous cure for impotence—it was permanently and powerfully erect.

When I was about ten, I suffered from anemia and resultant bouts of insomnia. An herb doctor instructed me to eat pigs' brains. Thinking back, I believe my doctor's prescription was based on at least two scientific premises:

1. Sleeping is a biological process controlled by the brain.
2. Pigs sleep well.

So Mother saved all the pigs' brains for me. Each morning she steamed a brain and carefully picked off all the veins. Then she lured and/or forced me to eat them. I hated them, but I ate them—by the hundreds. My pigheadedness today, according to the classical theory, must have some connection to those medicinal breakfasts of my childhood.

At night Mother lit her booth with an acetylene lamp. She dropped a block of acetylene into a bottle of water. Bubbles rose. The gas, trapped in the bottle, was siphoned off through a pipe and burned, emitting a dim glow and sooty smoke. And it stank.

One day I saw a kerosene lamp at a flea market. It was broken: the lid was missing and the pump leaked. The vendor wanted a quarter for it. I turned the lamp over and over in my hands, trying to make up my mind. I brought Bao in as a consultant. He could not decide, either. A quarter was a fortune. Finally, the salesman said we should buy it and try to fix it. If we couldn't get it to work, we could return it and get our money back. That clinched the deal.

My brothers and I tinkered secretly with that piece of junk for almost a week. And we fixed it! That evening Ling and I carried the lighted kerosene lamp, suspended from a shoulder pole, toward Mother's booth. I was in front; he was in back. The glare from the brilliant light blinded him.

"Wait!" Ling shouted. "I can't see!"

"Then close your eyes," I instructed my brother. "Just follow me."

Hanging the lamp created a sensation. Kids, attracted by the light, circled Mother's booth. With the spotlighted red pig's head in the center, the scene resembled a frantic tribal ritual.

A vendor's life is not an easy one. Profits are marginal and short-weighting is a common practice. But Mother's fingers were never deft, and she did not dare to cheat her customers. On the contrary, to keep her patrons happy she usually added an extra slice of meat to the package before wrapping it. Mother's honest business style, perhaps with the added attraction of the lamp, made her endeavor thrive. Starting with only half a pig's head, in less than a year she could easily sell two or three each night.

In 1956 the government deprivatized all small businesses. The Penglai District collectivized the pig's head meat sellers into one production team. Nine formerly private vendors were included. A converted hut served as the processing plant. Its bamboo walls were plastered with clay. A six-foot-high hardwood board was erected in front of the shabby door. On the board, in red, formal-style characters, was boldly carved:

CHINESE COMMUNIST PARTY
PENGLAI DISTRICT
PIG'S HEAD MEAT PRODUCTION TEAM BRANCH

Mother was permitted to join the team, and the whole family was happy.

As the saying goes, "The sparrow may be small, but it has all the necessary organs." The Penglai District Pig's Head Meat Production Team also had all the necessary parts: a party secretary, a political superintendent, a militia coordinator, a business director, and an accountant.

At the opening ceremony the party secretary addressed all of the employees. He explained the historical significance of deprivatization. He said that the pig's head meat business was becoming polarized. Some vendors were getting richer and richer while others were growing poorer and poorer. If this phenomenon was allowed to continue, exploitation, the source of all the evils of the old society, would return. Mother felt very guilty about her expanding business.

After collectivization, dehairing and cooking the meat became a group effort. Each vendor took a portion of the cooked meat and resold it in their own booth. The profits were shared equally.

The attic no longer stank of burned hair, and the steam from the "old soup" was quenched. But for some reason, after covering all the deductions and costs incurred by the new organization, Mother could no longer afford even the acetylene lamp. She resorted to candles. Every evening her lonely pig's head dozed in the dim, shaky light. Mother limped along in this way for two years. Then she resigned, citing the excuse of ill health.

She was finished with pigs.

Then she, like Wang Tian's mother before her, hired herself out as a live-in maid. She took my eight-year-old sister, Chuen, with her.

CHAPTER ELEVEN

Sheep Fat Soap

From the time I was a first grader until I graduated from middle school, there was always the odor of sheep meat lingering around my body. My classmates assumed I was a Muslim, but in fact, our family seldom ate mutton. The smell was the result of using sheep fat soap.

After leaving her first husband, my mother lived with her parents for ten years. She worked for my grandfather as an assistant in his successful soap factory.

When Mother married Father, my grandfather compiled all of his soap-making recipes and processes into a handwritten book. He gave the book to my mother as a wedding present. When I was young and learning brush-writing, Mother used grandfather's manuscript as one of my copybooks.

My grandfather's beautiful calligraphy really tormented his little grandson. It was a unique combination of Chinese characters and chemical symbols. The Roman letters written in formal-style brush strokes looked like the emperor's British tutor dressed in a Ching dynasty gown. In 1966, at the beginning of the Cultural Revolution, Mother destroyed the book along with other "remnants of the old society." Otherwise I would probably inflict the same pain on my own son.

North from our house, halfway to the Great World, was a butcher shop named the Shanghai Beef and Lamb Company. The shop window displayed beef and lamb, cooked and raw. Occasionally, by-products were put out for sale: tripe, hooves, heads, and tails. One day Mother brought back a whole basketful of sheep fat.

Sheep fat looks like beeswax and has a fine-grained texture, but its gamy smell is so strong that even Muslims seldom eat it. So the shop was happy to fill Mother's basket at a very low price.

Soap is the product of treating grease with lye, an extremely corrosive alkaline chemical. When my family first moved to Shanghai, Mother bought a whole box of lye, weighing about thirty pounds. The chemical had probably originally been U.S. Army materiel. Somehow it had ended up in a flea market alongside olive drab jackets, raincoats, canteens, and so on. The vendor had no idea what on earth was in the box. Mother was picking out a belt for me when she recognized the label that read NaOH.

The box must have been there for a long time; the tin had been partially eaten away by its contents. The vendor could stand the smell no longer, and he told Mother that if she bought the belt, she could take the whole box for nothing. My mother was thrilled and immediately sent me running home to summon Father. The two of them hauled the box back to the attic.

If rendering pork fat was unpleasant, then making soap was torture.

Mother dumped the sheep fat into a cauldron and built up the fire. When the grease had melted and its temperature climbed to around 100° C, she carefully added a weighed measure of lye, stirring constantly. Pungent yellow fumes burst forth, turning the attic into a hellhole. Father and Mother coughed and coughed. My brothers and I screamed as we watched. It was our curiosity that earned us our suffering— Mother had warned us ahead of time. We fled to the roof. Then Father, his nose dripping, carried my sister out after us. We left Mother to struggle in the inferno alone.

Many years later, when I was working in a truck repair factory, I again witnessed the power of lye. After dissecting an engine, the parts were put in a huge, square tank where they were boiled for hours to remove the greasy sludge. The liquid bubbling in the tank was nothing but a lye solution. I was assigned to design a sealed tank for this process, as quite a few operators' nasal membranes were being eaten through by the fierce fumes.

Five minutes after the lye was added to the hot grease, the fumes began to abate. The process of saponification required about twenty minutes of cooking. The paste got thicker and thicker. Its doneness was measured by its viscosity. Mother would dip a chopstick into the paste, lift it up, and watch it drip off. When it formed a thin, continuous stream, remaining unbroken to the end, it was ready. Mother would then take the cauldron off the fire and set it aside. As the paste cooled, it hardened into a milky-white block. That was soap. Then Mother flipped it out of the pot and onto the table. Using a thin wire, she sliced the block into small cakes and stored them in a wooden box.

Mother tried to sell her soap. Her tests proved that its washing power was as good as anything on the market. But unexpectedly, the gamy smell survived the heat and the violent chemical reaction, and drove away all potential customers. As a result, the six members of our family became the sole consumers of the sheep fat soap. For more than a decade, my family never bought a single piece of soap. Baths, dishwashing, laundry—we patriotically used our homemade product.

As an epilogue to this chapter, I'd like to bring an unusual biological phenomenon to the attention of entomologists all over the world. The attic harbored an army of bedbugs. They attacked us every night. They sucked our blood in the dark and left us itching and covered with red welts each morning.

For many years we tried every remedy available: DDT, Raid-X, Bug Death, Beetle-Gone . . . Few bedbugs were terminated, but two cats were sacrificed. Once my family began using sheep fat soap, however, the entire battalion of bedbugs miraculously retreated. And they never came back.

CHAPTER TWELVE

Rotten Fruit

An old saying goes, "Better to have one nibble of a fresh peach than to devour a whole bushel of rotten pears." It is sound hygienic advice and a valuable philosophical principle. In my case, however, I believe that my family's nutrition, and even our happiness, was closely linked with rotten fruit. As I write, North American lilacs blossom in the moonlight outside my window. But what the breeze brings me, wafting across thirty years, is the sweet, fermenting scent that rose from the heaped bamboo baskets and cattail bags of the fruit wholesaler on Penglai Road.

The Penglai fruit wholesaler was only about fifty yards from our home. It was a small shop, but it provided fruit for dozens of retailers in the area.

Fruit is seasonable merchandise. All winter and spring the wholesaler shut the doors and his employees, like a group of patient archaeologists, spent their days brushing the dust off a few dried dates. But in the fall, oh, my! Watermelons, honeydews, cantaloupes, apples, pears, bananas, persimmons, you name it, blew the wholesaler's doors wide open. The bins and shelves in the shop were packed and the fruit flooded out onto the sidewalk. The entire west end of Penglai Road became the wholesaler's domain.

The policeman controlling the traffic light at the intersection always gave the right-of-way to the overloaded trucks bringing in new supplies. Stopping and starting frequently tumbled the fruit from the trucks, and herds of children heedlessly chased them out into the streets.

I give many thanks to China's backward methods of fruit preservation. No matter how the produce was rushed from harvest to market, after it was tossed in ships, trains, and trucks, more than half would be rotten. The process of decay generously extended the pleasure of fruit consumption to families like ours.

The peach was the earliest fruit to come to market. Peaches, especially honey peaches, are very sensitive to pressure. Almost every willow basket, as it was unloaded from the truck, was dripping with juice. The winy scent of rotting peaches floated through the window and into our attic. Even if I was being suffocated by the rigid strokes of my calligraphy homework, my eyes would suddenly sparkle and I would call, "Mom!"

Mother must have smelled the fragrance, also. And she certainly knew that my excitement was not due to sudden enlightenment concerning the art of calligraphy. So she lifted up the corner of her blouse and extracted a ten-cent bill from the inside pocket. She took down a basket hanging from a beam and gave it to me.

"Watch out for trucks," she cautioned.

I grabbed the money. The bill, soggy from Mother's sweat

and warmth, crumpled itself into a ball in my hand. I dashed down the staircase. In a few seconds I arrived at the wholesaler's door. Actually, I had only arrived at the outer reaches of the fruit distributor's territory. The shop was surrounded by rank upon rank of bags, baskets, bushels, crates, and carts. I knew it was still early, so I sat on the curb across the street, watching for developments.

Understanding that the peaches on the top layers of the baskets suffered few casualties, I paid little attention when the store workers sorted them. But when they bent to reach the peaches on the bottom of the containers, I went on alert.

I didn't have to evaluate the status of each and every peach from my distant perch. I could assess their condition simply by studying a worker's movements. If the peach was good, he would carefully pick it up and carefully put it down. If it was rotten, he would casually toss it into a box, which became my target. When the box was full, I had to figure out in whose cart it was stowed.

I knew every retailer's cart. Even if they appeared identical to the unpracticed observer, I could identify each by the patch of rust on a handle or the dent on a frame. I didn't have to wait for the cart to leave. Instead, I went directly to the retailer who owned the vehicle. I didn't have to run; I had plenty of time.

Because my expertise was well recognized, I would be dogged by a number of other baskets. Most were carried by kids, a few by adults.

"Where? Where?" the kids would ask in a whisper, afraid the secret might leak. Sometimes I answered; sometimes I didn't. I whistled as I twirled my basket along the way.

The kids were very loyal. Even when they realized my destination, they seldom betrayed me. They followed me and willingly let me queue up ahead of them. The adults, however, were like jackals following lions. Their faces were solemn, as if they were planning to liberate Taiwan. I knew that they were trying to figure out to which fruit retailer I was heading. As soon as my goal was evident, they burned their bridges. Taking advantage of their long legs, they ran off, leaving the kids in their dust.

Usually I was tolerant of their blunt exploitation. A few adults in line ahead of us was not a big deal. But if I was not in a good mood or there were only a few peaches in the box, I would play a little trick. I would purposely lead them toward the wrong fruit retailer. Once the jackals had loped past, I knew that they wouldn't bother to look back. I would make a sharp turn and lead my pride of children to the real quarry. Sometimes my subordinates did not fully grasp my outflanking tactics, but they always followed me. I never disappointed them.

We queued up in front of the retailer's shop.

"What's coming?" the owner asked.

"Rotten peaches!" the kids crowed.

Then the owner would clean his tables, ready to welcome the coming bestseller. The line grew quickly. Some people asked; others didn't bother. If there was a line, there was sure to be a bargain.

When the cart came into view, a commotion would erupt in the line. The queue contracted into a mass. Fresh honey peaches usually cost thirty or forty cents a pound. Rotten, they were only five cents a pound at most. But you couldn't pick. The owner would pack them in a paper bag for you. Sometimes he weighed the bag; sometimes he didn't. Two pounds, more or less, was ten cents.

Even though the peaches were in paper bags, experience taught me that a basket was still necessary. After a couple of blocks, the bag would be soaked with peach juice and disintegrating rapidly. I often saw someone standing bewildered in the middle of the road, holding a dissolving bag of dripping peaches.

My biggest challenge, however, was getting the entire quantity home. I could easily eat as I walked. I wonder what power gave me the strength to resist temptation and bring all the peaches back to the attic. The only sample I tasted was the dripping juice. I caught it as it leaked out of the basket, and sucked the sweet liquid off my fingers. I think it must have been Mother's praise that gave me my willpower. When I returned home with a full load, she always made a big fuss. She would exclaim over my ingenuity in managing to get so many peaches for only ten cents. Mother's compliments gave me the impression that I was going to be promoted to minister of trade the next morning. I listened to her flattery a million times, but it never bored me. Mingled with the sweet scent of rotten fruit, it is a memory that will remain with me all my life.

After washing the peaches, Mother filled a basin with salt water, in which she soaked the fruit for about five minutes. I don't know if this sterilization technique is up to twentieth-century standards, but we never got diarrhea from the peaches.

Under my brothers' and sister's intense gazes, Mother took the biggest and best peach out of the water and handed it to me. I took the lion's share for granted. One huge bite and the juice was dripping from the corner of my mouth. Then Mother would choose the two next best peaches, place them in a bowl and cover them with gauze. They were for my father. Next came my sister's turn, then my two brothers'.

My brothers never complained about the obvious hierarchy. Maybe that was because Mother always put herself last. Sometimes when it came to her turn, Mother lifted the bowl and, like a magician, passed it above our eye level, placing it in the basket dangling from the beam overhead. Her invisible share hung suspended in the air.

There were times that Mother didn't have ten cents to give me. Then she waited until the fruit wholesaler closed for the evening. In front of the shop, she bent over the barrels and harvested the spoils. Quite often she returned with half a basket of something. Of course, the quality was worse. But after Mother's careful ministrations a bowl of colorful fruit salad would be presented for that night's dessert.

One day Mother returned with a full basket of pineapple peelings. She ground them into a pulp in a mortar. Then she put the pulp in a cotton flour sack and wrung out the liquid. That was the first time I ever drank pineapple juice.

In the United States pineapple juice is not expensive. You can buy a large can for a couple of dollars. But every time I drink pineapple juice, I see my mother holding her hands close to the light bulb, picking thorns out of her palms late into the night.

CHAPTER THIRTEEN

Father Was Old

Almost every Sunday during the few years that Father worked in the button factory, he took my brothers and me to the public bathhouse.

The button factory gave its workers coupons for baths, one coupon per day. Because our family lived upstairs from the factory, Father usually came home after work and just washed himself with a basinful of warm water. So the bathing coupons provided pleasure for his sons instead. The public bathhouse was not far away, about a twenty-minute walk. But I did not have to walk. I rode, rode high on my father's shoulders.

Riding on Father's shoulders was very prestigious. All of a sudden, I was much higher than my two brothers and my normal view of the chins of pedestrians switched to their scalps. The change of perspective gave me power and pride, like an Indian prince inspecting his subjects from the back of an elephant. The last time I rode on Father's shoulders, however, left me with a different memory.

I was eight then. I remember that it was the eve of National Day, and it was chilly. Mother laid out a sweater for each of her sons and urged us to put on our jackets as soon as we came out of the bathhouse. She said that the wind of fall was colder than the snow of winter, especially right after a hot bath when all your pores were open.

As usual, my brothers and I went downstairs first. We stood fidgeting on the sidewalk, impatiently waiting for Father. Whenever we were about to go out, the attic became unbearably cramped.

Finally Father came down. As was my routine, I turned my back to Father and spread my arms like wings. I was waiting for Father's hands to lift me from under my armpits. I would be powerfully launched high into the air and then gently lowered onto Father's shoulders.

Yes, here came the launch, and I was in the air, but far lower than the expected altitude. My feet hung only half a yard above the ground, frozen in the air, neither climbing up nor arcing down. In the next few seconds I felt only a trembling under my arms. Then I landed back on the sidewalk.

I turned around and looked up at my father, wondering what had happened.

Father looked bewildered. Bending slightly forward, he gazed at his hands as if extra fingers had sprouted from nowhere.

A few dead leaves rolled by his feet.

Sweat oozed from his forehead.

My two brothers stood at the intersection, waiting for us.

"I can walk by myself," I said, wanting to run to my brothers.

"Hold it." Father pointed to an old hydrant by the curb. "Climb up on that."

The hydrant was rusty but pretty big, with a platform on the top. I climbed onto it and stood up. Father stepped down from the curb and bent over. I opened my legs, and father's head moved in between them. My feet left the hydrant, and I rode on Father's shoulders.

I was riding toward the sun.

I held Father's head. It had been shaved a few days before and was already prickly. The sunshine seared my eyes. I looked down and saw my father's scalp. The hair had just sprouted out. So many hairs, white, glistening with tiny beads of sweat.

I must have seen those white hairs before, but I had never thought about what I had seen. I did not have to think about everything. Like a cloud passing by, like a willow swinging in the wind, a million things had slid through my pupils and never left a mark. They did not have to carry any specific meaning. Even if they did, it was not my business. But all of a sudden, I felt I had caught the elusive meaning of the white hair, and it was my business.

A drop of sadness seeped into my heart.

I rode on Father's shoulders, passing a market.

The market had just closed. The smell of fermenting vegetables, fish guts, wet chicken feathers, and rotten straw bags blended together, floating through the air. Elderly people, sitting in the dim teahouse, now and then emitted coughs muffled by the phlegm in their throats.

I thought of Ling's crickets.

There is a layer of fine hair on the neck of a young cricket.

As the autumn wind grew colder and colder, the hair of Ling's crickets got thinner and thinner. By the end of that fall, all the hair was gone, revealing the dark brown shells of their necks, as glossy as Father's scalp. You did not have to remember to close the lids all the time; the crickets could no longer jump out of their pots.

Sometimes in the night, an old cricket called, but long gone was his vigor and pride. His chirping sounded just like the coughs muted by phlegm.

The rice grain in his pot stayed untouched for a few days. Ling continued to add water to his peanut-shell cup, which only compensated for evaporation. Finally, one chilly morning, the roof tiles were covered with a heavy layer of frost. We opened the lid. The cricket was curled up in the corner, shrunken and dried.

A drop of the same sadness had seeped into my heart.

Bao and I once stealthily played with Father's button press. It was evening and the workshop was deserted. We put the plastic powder into the mold and Bao and I strained to propel the flywheel, but it didn't fly for us the way it did for Father. Instead, it shuddered its way down. A few minutes later we opened the mold. What we saw were not buttons, but a collection of chewed-up dregs. The worst part was that the dregs stuck in the mold and could not be dug out. Bao and I got a good beating for that unsuccessful experiment. Every time after that when I saw the flywheel flying under Father's muscles, I was awed.

When Mother made shoes for her sons, she made only one pair for each of us. She said we were changing every year. But when she made shoes for Father, she always made a few pairs. She said Father wouldn't change.

Yes, Father would never change.

The crickets would age and die every year, but Father's muscles would never shrink. The cranking of his press would shake the whole building forever. And forever I would be launched by Father, high up into the air.

But suddenly, my belief was shaken.

That day, after our baths, I walked home.

CHAPTER FOURTEEN

Crystal Radio

During my first year of middle school, I became addicted to crystal radios.

Crystal radios use copper sulfide to detect radio waves. Copper sulfide is a golden crystal; hence, the name crystal radio.

I made an exquisite box out of plywood. I used no nails, as they would have interfered with the radio waves. I painstakingly carved dovetail joints with a knife and put them together with ox-hide glue. After sanding, I painted it inside and out with white enamel to keep out any moisture, which would alter the radio's capacity. When it was finished, I tapped on the box; it sounded crisp. Good job!

Crystal radios do not require electricity, but the radio wave that activates the device is extremely weak. Therefore, resistance created by joints in the circuit must be minimized. The book said that for amateurs the wires could simply be twisted together, but all my joints were soldered like a professional's.

A soldering iron is a necessity for this work, but the price of a soldering iron lay far beyond my budget. I found a steel rod and filed off the rust. Heated on the stove, it became my soldering iron. For the flux I collected fluid from discarded batteries at the local garage. I knew that was sulfuric acid. I stripped the skins from dead flashlight batteries. The skins were zinc. I cut the zinc into small pieces and dropped them into the acid. A flurry of bubbles rose and I had zinc sulfide—a terrific flux.

There were ready-made crystal detectors for sale in the radio shop at thirty cents apiece. The price was unreasonable and I didn't trust the mass-produced merchandise. So I bought a chestnut-sized ball of copper sulfide from the amateur radio market. It cost me only ten cents. I broke the shiny ore into small grains. I carefully sorted them and chose three or four perfect crystal grains. I tested them one by one and, finally, put the winner in my radio.

No matter how hard you work to perfect your crystal radio, you cannot expect it to rattle a pair of twenty-four-inch speakers. But I was pretty happy with the results of my project. Late at night, when I hung my headphones on the wall beside my pillow, they squeaked as if a nestful of baby mice had taken up residence. Even my mother, sleeping at the other end of the attic, could hear it.

"Long-long," Mother would remind me, "turn off your radio when you are not listening to it. Don't waste electricity."

I giggled.

In those days, there were two radio stations transmitting in Shanghai. One broadcast in Mandarin, the official language of China, the other in the dialect of Shanghai. Including Radio Peking, which was rebroadcast locally, my little radio could receive three stations! Of course, the tuner, a wire coil wound around the paper cylinder, had its limits. Sometimes when Radio Shanghai's folk music was in high swing, Radio Peking's news cut in, with its distorted blah, blah, blah sounding like the arguing of the couple next door.

"Mixed-channel" broadcasting has its advantages, however. While the closing notes of the Peking opera soloist were dragged out indefinitely to impress the audience, a fanfare of brass would make an improvisational entrance, signaling other options on my dial.

As a middle school student, I had already outgrown whiny children's programs like "Golden Trumpet" or "Red Children." My favorite programs were "Cross Talk" (a comedy show) and foreign music.

In "Cross Talk" as it issued from the teasing lips of the comedians, the prestigious Chinese language acted like a naughty boy, totally forgetting its five-thousand-year history.

At that time the Soviet Union and China were still on their honeymoon. The outside world did not exist beyond their cloying embrace. So foreign music meant Soviet music, and Soviet music meant "The Hymn of Lenin," "The Hymn of Stalin," "The Hymn of the Fatherland," and so on. But at least it was exotic, quite different from Chinese music. After hearing them repeatedly, I could sing along, merrily rolling my r's.

Crystal sets derive all their energy from radio waves. The antenna functions not only as a signal receiver but also as the energy collector. The longer the antenna, the better.

In overpopulated Shanghai, crystal operators usually could only stick a spiderweb antenna out the window, randomly catching a few electrons that rashly stumbled into the snare. But

I was blessed. Thanks to my family's exclusive access to the roof, I could set up my antenna on its seventy-foot-long slope.

I first used steel wire. Steel wire can collect radio waves, but its high resistance severely reduces the efficiency of the whole circuit. Finally my chance came. An electric motor in the button factory on the ground floor burned out, and it needed to be recoiled. I enthusiastically volunteered to help the electrician take the burned copper wire out of the crevices. As my reward, the electrician allowed me to take home the spoils.

I braided the wire into a strand and attached a porcelain insulator to each end. I put up my "hi-tech" antenna on the roof. In the sunshine the insulator gleamed shiny white and the wire glittered gold. As soon as I had connected the antenna to the radio, the headphones roared.

One week after I installed the new antenna on the roof, Police Officer Chang climbed up to our attic. As usual, my father and mother waited respectfully for instructions. Unexpectedly, Officer Chang turned to me and said:

"You are the son of Cao Haichian, aren't you?"

"Yes, Officer Chang."

"Your name is Cao Guanlong, right?"

"Yes, Officer Chang."

"You can call me Comrade Chang. You are different from your parents."

"Yes, Com-comrade Chang."

"You are in the South District Middle School, aren't you?"

"Yes, Comrade Chang."

"Rumor has it that you have a radio. Is that correct?"

"Yes, Comrade Chang."

"How many electronic tubes? How many bands?"

"It's a crystal set." I pointed toward my pallet in the corner of the attic.

"Who made it? You, or your parents?"

"I did, Comrade Chang."

"Do your parents listen to it?"

"Let me think . . . uh, yeah, my mother listened once, but she said the headphones hurt her ears. After that she never listened to it."

"May I try it?"

"Of course!" I was excited. "Do you want to hear 'Cross Talk' or music? Right now it's six o'clock. Ah! You are lucky; 'Cross Talk' is on the air. Do you want me to tune it for you?"

"No, thank you." Officer Chang blocked my way. He bent over and crawled into the corner of the attic. His hat hit the ceiling beam and the visor was pushed awry. He lay down on my pallet, took off his hat, and put on the headphones. He tuned the dial back and forth for a long time. I was itching to know what he heard. Wouldn't it be wonderful, I thought, if I could listen to the radio with my brothers or friends, laughing at the same time, singing together? Since my new antenna was so powerful, I should definitely add another socket to my radio for a second set of headphones.

Finally, Officer Chang crawled his way out of the corner. I eagerly looked at him, waiting for his comments about what he had heard, but he did not say anything. He climbed up the ladder and stepped out the window onto the roof. He walked to and fro on the slope, inspecting my antenna. His polished, black leather boots broke several tiles.

Officer Chang reentered the attic, dusting off his hands. He adjusted his hat and asked me, "Do you know any foreign languages?"

"No."

"It is reported that you often sing foreign songs. Is that true?"

"Really? Oh, yeah! Those are Soviet songs. I don't know Russian really; I just sing along."

"Could you sing for me?"

"Oh, yes." Rumbling my r's as usual, I began to sing. Before I could finish a song, Officer Chang interrupted me:

"You sing very well. Your crystal radio is very good. May I borrow it for a couple of days?"

"Absolutely!" I was flattered. "If you want one, I can make one for you. I have a lot of leftovers. I have crystals. I have wire. I have . . ."

The next morning the house management company sent someone to replace the broken tiles. A few days later, the head of the residents' committee brought the crystal set back to me with a note:

> You are a smart boy. Though you could not choose your parents, you can choose your future. You are still reform-able. Stand on the side of the Party, follow the Party all your life.
>
> Comrade Chang

I put the note on the beam above my pillow. I lost track of how many times I read it. I felt warm and protected.

Worriedly, Mother watched as I put my radio back in its place. I continued to listen to foreign music; I continued to listen to "Cross Talk." I laughed when I got the jokes, startling Mother now and then. One day I, too, was startled.

That day at 7:00 P.M., there was foreign music as usual. I hastily shoveled rice into my mouth and crawled onto my pallet. I put on my headphones. The Moscow White Birch Song-and-Dance Ensemble was visiting China. Radio Peking was broadcasting its premier performance live. Just as the choir reached the middle of "Our Great Socialist Country," a burst of static whistled in my headphones, and a rich, baritone voice broke in:

"This is the Voice of America calling China. This is the Voice of America . . ."

Another burst of static and the voice disappeared.

I lay flat on my back, staring at a water stain on the ceiling.

The far side of the globe had always been shrouded in mystery. It was like looking down into a dark well: I had no proof of any material existence beneath the dancing reflections.

But abruptly, I heard its voice, if only for a few seconds. It was in my language, and it was such an impressive voice, confident and elegant!

I was mesmerized.

"Our Great Socialist Country" continued, but I no longer sang along. I couldn't help but lift my fingers to the dial. Carefully, I fine-tuned the radio, trying to catch that deep voice. But I heard only static floating in the ether. The voice had disappeared like a wraith.

I unplugged my headphones and hung them back on the nail. My eyes were opened wide, gazing at the black plastic casing of the ear pieces. Maybe it was the tension from tuning the dial; my fingers were trembling. The moonlight reflected off the wall and spread a shimmering mist around my pallet. The note still hung above my head, but I dared not read it again. The signature, "Comrade Chang," looked grim and pale.

Several weeks later my class from school went to the Penglai Movie Theater to see a film entitled *The Eternal Radio Wave.* The movie was about a communist spy who sent secret information from occupied Shanghai to Yan'an, then the inner-territory base of the Red Army. Eventually he was captured by the Japanese and executed.

The device used by the Japanese agent to intercept the clandestine broadcasts also revealed the location of his radio. After the movie, as we walked out of the theater, I thought: if that device could detect the location of a radio sending out messages, why couldn't it locate a radio that was receiving a specific broadcast?

I had often seen "Listening to the Enemy's Radio Broadcasts" listed as a crime on the posters that announced criminal convictions. The red crosses splashed on the posters vividly conveyed the finality of the executions.

Suddenly I was scared.

It was late evening when I got home after the movie. I climbed onto the roof in the dark. I grabbed the antenna. A single yank and the wire was broken. The porcelain insulator hit the tiles, emitting a crisp "ping!" Then I returned to the attic and crawled onto my pallet. I dragged down my radio. I pried the back of the set wide open. I stuck in my hand and grabbed the coil. I clenched my teeth and, with one swift pull, the radio became a gutted chicken.

That year I was twelve.

CHAPTER FIFTEEN

The Culture of Killing

Ever since I was quite young, I have heard and seen a colorful panoply of killing. Compared with the rich and profound techniques developed for killing *Homo sapiens* in ancient and contemporary China, my experiences are trivial and insignificant. But I still want to record them in this small book to make my humble contribution to the brilliance of Chinese civilization.

There are two methods of preparing eels for cooking. If the eels are thick, they are usually deboned alive. Eels are very slimy, so the amateur has difficulty with the job. But in the hands of the expert they meet a quick end.

The eel is clamped by the left hand, with the middle finger above and the index and ring fingers below. An awl pins the eel's head to the board below. A long stroke of the right hand smoothes the writhing eel. Simultaneously, a razor held between thumb and index finger of the right hand cleanly fillets the left side from neck to tail. Another slash of the razor, and the eel is left a whip of white bones. The mouth still gently spills bloody foam.

The meat from eels that are butchered alive is tender. In most cases, however, eels are given a hot shower before they are prepared. The eel vendor does not provide his own boiling water. Hot water shops are commonly built adjacent to a marketplace. The vendor carries a half-bucket of eels to the hot water shop and places it under the tap.

"Is the water ready?" he asks.

The operator of the boiler nods his head.

With a yank, the vendor opens the tap and a thick column of steaming water pours into the bucket.

All the eels get excited.

The wooden bucket is well designed, with a wide bottom and a small mouth—no eel is able to jump out. The eel carnival lasts only a few seconds; then the commotion subsides. A mound of foam lingers on the rim like the head on draft beer.

There are also two ways to terminate rabbits. For the common rabbit, simply grab its hind legs and, with a quick swing, hit its head on a cement floor. But the long-haired rabbit requires special treatment.

Long-haired rabbits are used for fur. The furrier usually checks the quality of the pelt by grasping the hairs between his fingers and combing through them. The fewer hairs that are shed, the better the fur. The following procedure is specifically designed to strengthen the adherence of the hair to the skin.

A steel bar, one inch thick, a foot and a half long, is prepared.

One end is filed smooth and round, the other end is fixed in a wooden handle. The bar is heated on a stove. When it glows red, the rabbit is taken out of its cage and put on the table. The furrier caresses the rabbit's back. Feeling soothed and comfortable, the rabbit lifts its tail. At the split second the anus is exposed, the bar is plunged in. The rabbit's mouth opens. Before a sound can escape, the poker protrudes from between its teeth. The unique stimulation makes every pore contract, clutching each hair in a death grip.

I never saw with my own eyes a banquet where they served White Jade of the Golden Monkey. I read about it in a musty antique recipe at the book flea market near the Temple of Letters. Under the title there was a line drawing, in characteristically warped perspective, depicting the construction of a special table.

The table was built in two halves with a hole in the middle. The head of the monkey emerged through the hole, with its neck clamped by the two sides. It could breathe, but it could not retract its head. A couple of bars were installed beneath the table, as a perch for the sacrifice.

It was the exotic illustration that held me. Confronting the brain-wrenching classical Chinese, I squatted at the stall. Retrieving all the rusty vocabulary that my mother had stuffed into my head from the "Imperial Essays," I eventually deciphered the recipe.

First, the book instructed, the guests must bathe in water infused with jasmine petals. The tableware and utensils had to be fashioned of pure silver. I remember a line of the recipe that read:

Only with clear mind, only with pure silver, can the soul of
the monkey be adopted into thy heart.

When the monkey was in position, a ladleful of hot oil was
sprinkled on its head. The hair was thereby loosened and easy
to pull out. Care had to be taken when pouring the oil so as not
to burn the ears and eyes of the monkey. The book decreed:

The ears and eyes of the golden monkey are portals. The
spirit of heaven and earth enter through them, and in the
brain foregather. No damage should be done.

The dehairing could be assigned to an assistant, but the
breaking of the skull had to be performed by an expert. The
monkey's head was struck with a silver hammer. The force had
to be precise. If the blow was too gentle, the skull would remain
intact. If it was too strong, the monkey would be knocked out,
or even worse, the "white jade" under the scalp might be
smashed.

When the skull was broken, the shards were carefully picked
out with silver tweezers. Then the membrane had to be peeled
off. Extreme caution had to be taken—the membrane was
tightly wrapped around the brain. If the brain was accidentally
broken, the juices would escape. That was called "leaking the
heavenly secret" and meant the dish was ruined. When the
membrane had been removed, the "white jade" was presented
to the distinguished guests.

At this point, the monkey was still conscious. Its eyes glittered, looking around at all the guests. The diners, in contrast,
closed their eyes in meditation, waiting for the most sacred

moment—"jade breaking." (I believe the term had been appropriated from classical novels where it suggested the taking of a maiden's virginity.)

Breaking the "jade" was a great honor, and the ritual was performed by the oldest or highest-ranking guest. The spoon designed for jade breaking was very small, only the size of a peanut shell, but the handle was twice as long as a regular spoon's.

The honored guest slowly extended the spoon toward the "jade." A slight tap, and the brain oozed out.

He scooped a half spoonful of "jade" and solemnly brought it to his lips. Closing his eyes, he savored the taste from the tip of his tongue to the back of his palate. Then he emitted a long sigh. He opened his eyes, his pupils shining. He looked around at everyone gathered at the table.

A hubbub arose.

Starting from the jade-breaker and moving around the table from east to west, the guests tasted the delicacy, one by one. The sequence from east to west was crucial. If the direction of rotation was incorrect, the energy of the universe would turn into evil fire, driving the diners insane. Weird as it sounds, modern medicine recognizes a similar pathological condition in New Guinea called laughing disease, or kuru. It results from eating raw, infected brains.

Small world.

Live Fish Feast is a famous dish in Nanjing, the former capital of the Nationalist government. The only people who can afford to consume it are senior leaders or foreign guests. It is not that the fish is rare; any freshwater fish such as carp or trout is good enough. Rather, it is the involved cooking process that makes the feast a lofty endeavor. In all of Nanjing, only two or three chefs are qualified to prepare the dish.

In February 1972 President Nixon visited China. At a press conference in Shanghai, a reporter in his entourage abruptly asked an out-of-the-blue question:

"Is Live Fish Feast considered a remnant of the old society?"

Perhaps he was just trying to show off the knowledge he had gleaned from a dust-covered book the night before he left for his assignment. But the Chinese government took it very seriously. The Foreign Ministry dispatched a chef by helicopter from Nanjing to Shanghai. In the Foreign Guest House restaurant, the chef demonstrated Live Fish Feast.

The Central Documentary Movie Company shot the whole procedure in color. The film was distributed worldwide to prove that, in the midst of the Cultural Revolution, China still took good care of its cultural traditions.

The movie began with a close-up of a fish tank. A few plump carp swam gracefully in the water. Then the lens tilted up and a chef approached the tank. With a big smile, he stuck his hand into the water and pulled out a carp.

Close-up: the fish flapped its tail, splashing drops of water.

Fade-in: the kitchen. A smoking pot of oil on the stove. The chef swiftly scaled and gutted the fish. Inserting two fingers into the gills, he dipped the body of the fish into the hot oil. The whole movie theater vibrated with the sound of sizzling oil, 120 decibels, fully expressing the intensity of the heat. The fish's head remained suspended by the chef, one inch above the surface of the oil. The gills still pulsed in the smoke.

The deep frying took only two or three seconds. Then with a flourish, the fish was flung onto a white, oval platter.

The complicated sauce was prepared well in advance: dried lily flower, wood ear fungus, wild mushrooms, shrimp extract, sesame oil, coriander, ginger, garlic, and more. One flash of the ladle and the whole fish was colorfully dressed.

A long pan shot brought the carp to the table.

A round of cheers was followed by an air raid of chopsticks.

Close-up: the body of the fish had already become a skeleton, but the head remained fresh. The eyes still sparkled. The mouth still murmured . . .

There are virtually no taboos in the gamut of Chinese food. Almost anything can be turned into a delicacy. Of things with two wings, airplanes are the only exception. Of things with four legs, only benches are pardoned. Not only do we eat anything, but we eat it with a unique twist. The consumption of two kinds of birds provides examples.

Deep-fried sparrow is a popular game dish. It's not difficult to catch sparrows. In the evening, when the sparrows have gone to roost in the shrubs, large nets are hung in front of the bushes. Then, behind the nests, a gong is suddenly beaten. The startled sparrows fly out and crash into the net. With their wings entangled in the threads, they can easily be picked out, one by one.

The tricky part is getting rid of the feathers.

Sparrows have fragile skin. If the bird is plucked after it is dead, the skin will come off with the feathers. Sparrows are small to begin with; if you lose the skin how much is left? So sparrows are usually plucked alive.

Defeathering live sparrows is labor intensive. But at least their cheeping and the constant fluttering of their wings in your hands relieve some of the monotony.

I remember when I was a sixth grader, one of the third-place winners of the annual Grammar School Invention Contest was a classmate of mine. I no longer can recall his proper name, but everyone called him Black Skin. Black Skin's invention was the Easy Pigeon Terminator.

It was a citywide contest, so winning third place was a big honor. Proudly, the school officials called a grand assembly for Black Skin to lecture on his invention.

Black Skin said his father was a chef in a game restaurant, and red-cooked (stewed in soy sauce) pigeon was one of his specialties. Black Skin told us that his father had once asked him to help kill pigeons. Black Skin Sr. told Black Skin Jr., and Black Skin Jr. told us, that the pigeons were not supposed to be killed with a knife. If the blood drained out, the meat would taste dry and tough.

Black Skin took a live pigeon from a bamboo cage under the podium and started his demonstration. First he showed us the traditional method. He held the bird in his left hand. With his right thumb and index finger, he tightly covered the two breathing holes above the beak. The pigeon began to struggle. The spasms gradually subsided. Black Skin released his fingers, and the pigeon revived.

Black Skin said you had to cut off the bird's air supply for at least five minutes to finish it. The day he worked for his father, Black Skin killed twenty pigeons in a row. His fingers became flattened and trembled for two days. The tedious work inspired his invention.

Then Black Skin showed us his award-winning machine. The Easy Pigeon Terminator was definitely easy to use. It consisted of two clips linked together. One clip held the beak from above and below. The other clamped the air holes from left and right. The ends of the clips were rubber-tipped to better seal out the air.

Black Skin plugged the pigeon into his device and tossed it onto the stage. Flapping its wings, the pigeon tried to take off, but the clips were attached to a cast-iron block. So, dragging its head, the bird performed a bizarre dance on the stage.

Finally it calmed down.

This time Black Skin did not let it revive.

There is a famous dish in Yunnan Province called Baby Mice.

Keep a cage full of female mice, mate them to a male mouse, and a continuous supply of baby mice is guaranteed. A baby mouse is only as big as the last segment of your little finger. Pink. No hair.

One serving of Baby Mice consists of four infants. The squirming babies are put in a small gilded-porcelain dish and brought to the table. Simultaneously, a dish of sauce is served: mustard, wild pepper, soy sauce, sesame oil, white vinegar, brown sugar, and so on. The list of ingredients is complex, and every restaurant has its own secret recipe. But eating the baby mice is always simple. You just pick one up with pointed, ivory chopsticks and drop it in the sauce. It rolls and wiggles, coating its body with all the spices. Then you pick it up again, and pop it in your mouth.

Chew and chew.

While Baby Mice describes one dish's contents, the meaning of Purple Strips is difficult to guess. Purple Strips was a therapeutic food in Guangxi Province, which borders Vietnam. The primary ingredient was a young cow, around one year old, having just reached puberty but not yet been mated.

The young cow was led to the edge of a pond. The pond appeared quite ordinary, just a regular fish pond. But there were no fish in it. Instead, in the mud under the water, millions of leeches lay in ambush.

Instinctually the cow felt that something was wrong. She kicked her hind legs and tried to retreat. But she could not withstand the whips laid across her buttocks for long, and gradually she waded into the water. The army of leeches that had been waiting impatiently in the mud swarmed out and latched onto every part of the cow.

In five or six minutes, the owner dragged the cow back out of the water. Her whole body was covered with leeches. With a thin, bamboo blade, he scraped the already engorged leeches into a wooden bucket.

Though he did not wear a watch, the owner had to have a good sense of timing. If the session was too short, the leeches would not have siphoned enough blood. If it was too long, they would have sucked their fill and contentedly fallen off into the water.

After the first leech harvest was complete, the owner drove the cow back into the pond. The process was repeated again and again.

As the volume of leeches in the bucket increased, the cow's blood was being draining away. Eventually, the owner led the withered cow to the butcher shop where she was slaughtered. The womb was saved for later use.

The leeches had enjoyed their warm blood banquet for some

time; now it was their turn to contribute. When a cauldron of water reached a rolling boil, the leeches were dumped in. They were instantly scooped out and chilled in cold water. Once removed from their cold bath, they were spread on a wide bamboo sieve to drain. Women sitting around the sieve slit each leech lengthwise with sharp, pointed blades and turned it inside out. Then they picked out a coagulated cow's blood strip with the tip of their knife and dropped it into an iced jar where it was reserved.

Traditional Chinese medical theory assumes that a woman's infertility is the result of low *chi,* or energy, in the blood. Cow's blood can aid the *chi,* but it is too hot. Taken directly, the heat can linger in the woman's body for many months, leading to prolonged bleeding after she gives birth. Leeches, residing in mud at the bottom of brooks or ponds, have a *yin,* or cool, nature. Once the cow's blood is sucked by the leeches, the *yang* of the blood is instantly balanced by the *yin* of the leeches. The heat is significantly quenched, yet the energy remains. Hence, the miraculous, therapeutic effect of Purple Strips, which enhances the blood energy in a cool fashion.

Even better, the spirit of the leeches can contribute their unique elasticity to the woman and help her withstand intense expansions and contractions during her long labor.

Yet a dose of Purple Strips was extremely expensive. Ordinary women from farmers' families dared not even think of it. Only a few ladies from aristocratic families could afford the cure.

To prepare a proper dose, the cow's womb was thinly sliced. Accompanied by wild ginseng, yellow angelica, black longans, red dates, shark fins, and swallows' nests, the womb soup was simmered all night. The Purple Strips were not removed from the iced jar until the moment of serving. They were submerged in the simmering broth, and almost immediately the pot was removed from the stove. Never overcook the Purple Strips. Even a few seconds' delay will totally ruin the treasure—the active energy, stored in the blood, will shrivel and die out.

While surveying or studying primitive cultures of the past and present, it is not unusual for archaeologists or anthropologists to bump into isolated achievements so advanced that no satisfactory explanation can be made for their origins. The Red Petals described below serves as an example.

Like many Asian ethnic groups, villagers living in the cloud-shrouded Daliang Mountains in the deep south of Sichuan Province were fond of dog meat. It was their unique slaughtering process, however, that earned the esteemed reputation of their Red Petals dog meat.

As with Purple Strips, Red Petals derived its name from blood—in this case, dog's blood. Dog's blood is even hotter than cow's blood; consuming it will give the eater an instant nosebleed. The only use for dog's blood was to splash it on an enemy's statue in a ritual curse before a tribal fight—to burn the evil to death. Since such rituals were not a frequent practice, most of the blood had to be discarded.

But blood is the stream that carries nutrition, and it is a shame to throw out the baby with the bath water. Some researchers have therefore assumed that the unique slaughtering process used to produce Red Petals dog meat was developed to save the nutrition while disposing of the waste.

Two sticks were employed in the procedure. One stick stretched the dog's forelegs wide open; the other stretched the hindlegs. In this cruciform position, the dog was skinned alive. Then the dog was released from the sticks and allowed to roam freely in the enclosed pit of the slaughterhouse.

The naked dog wouldn't bark. Like a drunk, he slowly and quietly walked around the pit, one circle after another. His staring white eyeballs never blinked—there was nothing to blink with. Blood was seeping out from his exposed muscles, dripping along his staggering legs. Red petals were blooming under his paws. It took at least ten minutes before the dog finally collapsed.

There is a significant difference between the conventional throat-slashing slaughtering and the flaying-alive process. In the first practice, all the nutrition is flushed away with the blood through the cut artery. But in the latter method, the blood is forced to sieve through all the capillaries while the nutrition carried by the warm liquid is filtered and reserved by the billions of cells of the dog's flesh.

CHAPTER SIXTEEN

The Milk Incident

The image of Police Officer Chang was sacred.

He was tall and thin, and he walked with a measured tread. Seen from behind, his buttocks were as flat as his clipboard. Two creases cut straight down from his waist right to the heels of his shoes.

In the summer, the baking sun turned the asphalt sticky. Telephone poles writhed like pythons in the steaming currents that rose in the wake of the sprinkler tank truck. But Officer Chang, his jacket still buttoned up to his neck, carried his clipboard and walked with the same measured tread in the vibrating air. Catching a glimpse of his white uniform approaching in the distance, the naked children playing in the spray of an open hydrant would scatter. The dripping youngsters hid around the corner in the lane until his round hat disappeared into the distance. Then they cheered and returned to their splashing.

Unexpectedly, Officer Chang's sacred image was spoiled by a few drops of milk.

Officer Chang's wife was a nurse in the block's health booth. Every afternoon, from one until five, she busied herself with Merthiolate and Mercurochrome, thermometers and blood pressure cuffs. But her primary implement was the syringe. The patients on the block brought ampoules of medicine from the hospital to her booth, where the shots were administered. It was convenient and inexpensive.

Mrs. Chang wore thick glasses, so thick that when she looked through them at an angle, the bottles on the wall shelves flattened out completely. But she was very good at injections. She gave me a few shots. She scratched my rear end with her fingernails, and before I noticed anything, the needle had already been withdrawn. Mrs. Chang sometimes helped me with my belt, always insisting I tuck in my shirttails—if I happened to be wearing a shirt.

In the morning Mrs. Chang was in charge of milk distribution for the block. Of the approximately three thousand families living on our block, only about fifty could afford milk. The dairy would deliver the fifty bottles to the health booth each morning. Then Mrs. Chang would load them into her pushcart and deliver them door to door.

My family, of course, was not among the lucky fifty, but each morning when I saw her on the street, I would greet her, "Good morning, Mrs. Chang." Her eyes, which seemed to be peering through the wrong end of binoculars, smiled at me from far, far away.

One morning I noticed someone else was delivering the milk.

I saw the women of the block gathered in clusters, gossiping in whispers. Rumors were running wild, creating a sensation.

The word was: Mrs. Chang had stolen milk.

It was hard to believe. The milk bottles were securely sealed. How could she possibly have stolen any? Rumor said that every morning, with her thinnest hypodermic needle, Mrs. Chang discreetly pierced the waxed paper lid of each bottle and removed one or two milliliters of milk. In this way she could collect a half cup of milk each day.

But how could such a tiny hole have been discovered? People said that a doctor living in Penglai Lane had found a few ants congregated on the lid of his unopened milk bottle. Curious, he examined the lid and found the tiny hole. He did not make a fuss, but continued checking the milk bottle lid for the next six mornings and found six holes. So he brought the lids to the dairy company.

That was all rumor. I was not sure if it was true or not. But it was true that Mrs. Chang no longer delivered the milk. And it was also true that Mrs. Chang no longer gave injections.

Moreover, the unlicensed vendors of fruit, ice pops, and shoe shines dramatically changed their attitudes. Formerly, they would run off like rabbits whenever Officer Chang approached. Now they stood their ground, conducting business as usual. The ice pop vendor thumped on his wooden box even louder and, with an outstretched neck, he shouted:

"M-i-i-l-l-k ice pops!"

The fruit vendor, with lowered head, casually threw a long apple peeling right under Officer Chang's feet.

Officer Chang didn't hear anything.

Officer Chang didn't see anything.

Wearing his white hat, wearing his white uniform buttoned up to his chin, Officer Chang moved on. The clipboard was still under his arm; the creases still cut from his waist to his heels. He walked with the same measured tread until his silhouette dissolved into the shimmering air.

Soon after, Mrs. Chang moved and Officer Chang was transferred. Nobody knows where they made their next home.

CHAPTER SEVENTEEN

Relocation

Early in 1958 a storm of population relocation swept through Shanghai. Everywhere, tables, chairs, pots and pans, jars and boxes lay scattered on street corners and sidewalks. If you did not see the "For Sale" signs, you would think that a typhoon had just hit the city.

Jobless residents and people with political problems were the primary targets of the government's enforced relocation. The city's population had been expanding rapidly, and the availability of food and housing had dwindled. In addition, the turmoil caused by rightists in 1957 demonstrated that Shanghai, with its complex colonial history, badly needed another housecleaning. My parents met the two criteria: they had no formal job and they were landlords in exile. So it was not surprising when our family was put on the list for relocation.

We were assigned to a place named Ningxia, which meant Summer Peace. When we received the notification, my parents had no idea where Ningxia was. The name had a strong southern flavor. But upon opening our atlas, we discovered that Ningxia was an Autonomous Muslim Region in Qinghai Province, bordering on Mongolia. Our atlas included short paragraphs describing the local customs and geographic features of each province. A Song dynasty poem was quoted to summarize the image of the remote territory:

Wind like daggers,
Snow like platters,
A yak bending over
On and on he lumbers.

Our family would be accepted by a farm called New Life. It was a labor reform farm. But the police told my parents that we were not being sent there for reform. Some of the convicts on the farm had completed their sentences and remained there to work. The members of my family would be like them, enjoying all the political rights of citizens.

Almost as rampant as the sidewalk furniture sales were the colorful recruiting posters plastered on the telephone poles: Shandong coal mine, Shanxi iron mine, Guizhou tea farm, Inner Mongolia cement factory, Yunnan marble quarry . . . Recruiting agents from all corners of China crowded the third- and fourth-class restaurants of Shanghai. The relocation campaign was a good chance for them to grab a handful of well-educated workers from the city with the highest literacy level in China.

Shanghainese are somewhat agoraphobic. They will never voluntarily pull out their roots from the warm, cozy marsh on which the metropolis was built. Someone even borrowed a Communist martyr's poem to describe their determination.

The original ran:

My blood can be shed,
My head can be cut off,
But my belief in Communism
Can never be lost.

Their version was:

My blood can be shed,
My head can be cut off,
But my residency in Shanghai
Can never be lost.

In the relocation campaign, however, you were better off forgetting the revised poem. You could keep your head and your blood, but you had to leave, period. You had no control in determining your destination. If you preferred to sign up with the recruiters, though, you had some say in where you went and what you did.

All the recruiting agents were having a good time. They set up long lines of tables in the lobbies, dining rooms, and hallways of their hotels, each team displaying a recruiting banner. Flapping their forms with both hands, squawking and shouting, they resembled a flock of seagulls following a boat's wake, scrambling for the refuse dumped over the stern.

In the summer of 1957 my oldest brother, Bao, graduated from high school and did not get into college. He had often thought of leaving Shanghai to try his luck elsewhere. This idea was absolutely rejected by my parents. They said that our family had worked so hard to settle down in Shanghai, staying together through thick and thin, that things would surely get better in the future. But when we got the relocation notice, my parents' attitude changed abruptly. Father quit his cart pushing, and Mother abandoned her pigs' heads. They spent their days wandering the streets from one telephone pole to the next, copying recruitment information.

One evening Father and Mother spread all the names and addresses they had collected on the dinner table. With five heads clustered under the lightbulb, we started our frantic journey. Flying from the northern border directly to the southern fringe, rocketing from the western mountains and splashing down on the east coast, we stayed hopped up until late at night. My little sister, however, curled up under the table and fell asleep.

Early in the morning of the following day, my parents dragged their three sons out of bed. Mother prepared a bowl of noodles topped with a poached egg for each of us. We were sweating after the big meal. Then Mother gave Bao the sheet of addresses chosen the night before and a dollar bill. She told Bao to take his two younger brothers on his search for a way out. Ling and I were a little worried—Father's stick never spared us when we cut class.

"What about school?" we asked.

"Forget about that!" Father slammed his fist on the table and roared.

My parents had forgotten about everything. Their only concern was to find a way for their three sons to escape. Anywhere would be okay, any job would be fine, as long as it was not on the New Life farm.

Bao was old enough for recruitment, but Ling was only sixteen and I, thirteen. How Mother wished that even my seven-year-old sister, Chuen, could be recruited, too!

The recruiters wouldn't give you a form unless they thought you showed promise. Bao was big and, with the added attraction of a high school diploma, he collected many forms in just one morning. But Ling had trouble; he was still two years shy of the hiring age. He struggled for half a day and didn't get a single form. And I was entirely out of range. Every time I elbowed my way to the tables, I was swept aside before I could open my mouth.

At noontime Bao bought three rolls of scallion crackers. We discussed the morning's results as we ate. Ling was clearly depressed. Maybe it was the whole morning's ignominies; a spontaneous, revolutionary urge burst out of me.

"Damn it!" I slapped Ling on the back of his head and said, "You look so old I bet you can easily pass for my grandfather. Why don't you just say you're a couple of years older?"

Startled, Ling looked up at Bao. A "hmmph" issued from Bao's nose, but he didn't give any explanation as to what the "hmmph" meant. After lunch we wiped our mouths and marched toward the next hotel.

By then I knew I had no chance. It was only for fun that I followed my brothers through the crowds. Again Bao got a form in a few seconds, but he didn't leave. He took out the wad of forms from the morning's search and waved them in the recruiter's face.

"Look, I want someone who can take me and my brother at the same time. See, this is my brother," Bao patted Ling on his head. "Good stuff! Smart, obedient, never gets sick, and he eats much less than I do."

The recruiters laughed.

"But," Bao continued, "there is a small problem. Maybe I

shouldn't call it a problem. My brother is only a few weeks short of his birthday. You know, you pick fruits when they are green, and by the time they get to the market, they are ripe. Well, what do you think?"

Watching, I almost cheered!

Ling, like a freeloader caught on a bus, did not dare to raise his head. The recruiter looked him over from head to toe, then whispered to the man sitting next to him. Finally he gave a form to Ling!

Two weeks later the Steel Company of Gansu Province took my two brothers away.

Before we said farewell, the whole family went to a photography studio to have a group portrait taken. The six-inch family portrait hung beside the picture of the Bodhisattva for eight years. It was taken down and destroyed, along with the Bodhisattva, in the winter of 1966, the beginning of the Cultural Revolution. But I still remember every detail of the portrait sharply.

Father sat in the middle. At that time he was sixty, with heavy bags under his eyes, but his newly shaven scalp was still tight and shiny. He wore a pair of wrap-around Chinese pants. They must have been overstarched—the wrinkles looked more like tin than fabric. Father wore the black cloth shoes Mother had made for him. Under their thick soles you could see part of the horseshoes that had been added for reinforcement. Father had piercing eyes. Even when he reached eighty and suffered from cataracts, the whitened pupils still glittered. But in that portrait his eyes looked lost.

Mother sat on Father's left side with my sister, Chuen, on her lap. It must have been the result of the photographer's flirting: the little girl smiled, revealing two missing teeth. Mother's hair, shiny and black, was neatly combed back into a bun. Her expression was calm and solemn. Mother was forty-seven then but still had elongated eyes and curving brows. She still looked like a palace lady in a Tang painting.

I stood beside Mother, wearing a woolen pullover. The camera lens must have been very sharp—if you looked carefully you could see the variety of old yarn that made up my sweater. To compensate for my thin eyes, I lowered my chin and rolled up my eyelids. I was trying to imitate the sophisticated look of popular actors' publicity photos. But it didn't work. It only added a few wrinkles to my forehead.

Bao wore a short-sleeved sailor's T-shirt, his muscles rippling under the stripes like a zebra's. He stood heroically behind Father, with his left hand draped over Ling's shoulder. Bao was confident that he had the power to provide full protection for his brother, wherever they went, whatever happened.

Ling stood beside Father, his back curved slightly. His hair was neatly combed. He looked like a docile assistant in an antiquated herb shop. Among us three brothers, he was the most concerned with his appearance. Every time we passed a window, he turned his head toward the glass, breathed on his palm, and smoothed his hair.

Mother paid extra for quick prints. Bao and Ling each got a copy of the family portrait before their departure.

Ling stayed in Gansu for about five years. In 1963 the steel company disbanded for lack of ore. Ling, by then a licensed electrician, was reassigned to Xian, an ancient city in the middle of China. There he worked in a grain shop, selling rice and wheat flour, liking his job as usual.

Another twelve years passed. In 1976 Father died. Ling was eagerly pursuing Party membership. Afraid that his coming back for our landlord-father's death would endanger his political future, we didn't inform him of the news until a month later. Ling came home on his vacation. His neatly combed hair had disappeared from the top of his head, leaving a scalp as shiny as Father's had been.

We four siblings were reunited. We sat around Mother. Above our heads was still the slanted attic roof; beneath our legs was still a pallet.

"Don't be sad," Mother said. "Heaven blessed us. Your father and I lived twenty years longer than we deserved."

We kept silent. We didn't know what Mother meant.

"Do you still remember that family portrait?" Mother asked. We nodded.

"Your father and I should have been dead soon after it was taken," Mother said. "That portrait was for you children to remember us by."

Mother told us that she and Father had prepared everything. She had prepared a set of clean clothes for Father, and she had prepared a set of clean clothes for herself. All the letters were written, stamped, and sealed. One letter was to her father in Hunan, the only relative with whom we corresponded. One letter was to Bao and Ling, addressed to the Steel Company of Gansu Province, where my two brothers were headed. The last letter was to the Shanghai Orphanage. In that missive, Mother listed the merits and weaknesses of my sister and myself.

Mother especially mentioned the scar on my sister's left arm, the result of the hot grease accident. Mother said the scar just looked bad; it didn't impair Chuen in any way. She asked the orphanage to inform the prospective families who were willing to adopt us.

The day before my brothers left, Father broke the rusty lock on a wooden box. A few tins of left-over lye were stored in the box. Mother bought two bowls with extra-thick walls in which to prepare the lye solution. My parents were determined to use the soap-making chemical to bleach out their dirty ties to the two youngest children still bound to them.

I remember the day we said good-bye to my brothers at the North Train Station. Afterward, my parents took my sister and me to the Golden Restaurant. We enjoyed a real feast. I forget how many dishes we ate. The thing I remember is that Mother kept picking out the shrimp from her noodles and giving them to Chuen and me.

"Ridiculous," Father said to Mom. "Why don't you just buy another dish of shrimp noodles?"

After we left the Golden Restaurant, Father and Mother brought us to the Heavenly Pond, a high-class public bathhouse that we had never aspired to visit before. Mother took Chuen into the ladies' section, and Father took me into the gentlemen's section. I remember that the steaming towels served to us smelled wonderful.

Coming out of the bathhouse, Mother gave me a fifty-cent bill. She asked me to go to the movies with my sister. I don't recall what movie we saw that day. I only remember that Chuen and I each had a lollipop, and we sucked them all the way home.

They tasted so good that we almost forgot our two brothers were heading far away on the clattering train.

As soon as my sister and I stepped into the attic, Mother clutched us. With one arm hugging me, the other squeezing Chuen, Mother knelt trembling.

Father handed a piece of paper to me. He had found it when they came back from the bathhouse. It had been stuck in the gap of the attic door. I looked at it. It was a notice from the Public Security Bureau. It said:

AFTER DELIBERATION, THE COMMITTEE FOR
POPULATION RELOCATION HAS DECIDED TO CANCEL
THE ORDER CALLING FOR YOUR FAMILY'S
EVACUATION.

Finished with her story, Mother sat on the pallet, facing the north window, focused on nothing.

Wind came.

The loosened roof tiles rattled above our heads. We never heard that kind of sound when we were young.

Old. Even the attic was getting old.

We four siblings wept quietly in commemoration of our father. Though he was a landlord, though he beat us, he was still our father, a kind father.

More than twenty years have passed since the relocation campaign. As to why we were suddenly allowed to remain in Shanghai, no one ever gave us any explanation. It was not necessary to give any explanation, anyway.

About a year after the storm of relocation, a few families who had been displaced reappeared on the streets. Mother knew some of the women. In chatting, she learned that the organizations outside Shanghai had needed laborers. But among the relocated families there were many "garbage" people—the old, the babies, the sick, the disabled. So the "cheated" organizations swept the junk back.

Maybe it was Father's age that saved us. Maybe it was my sister's age that saved us.

And maybe it is better not to guess at all.

CHAPTER EIGHTEEN

Automotive School

I still wonder why my parents so stubbornly hoped that a college student would emerge from our family. Was it a belief that higher education or professionalism could provide extra protection for their children? Or was it simply a kind of vain fantasy to soothe the pain and shame of being exiled from their homeland?

The most advanced scholar in Father's village had been a middle school graduate. The day the scholar came home, his father, the owner of a local tissue paper mill, butchered a buffalo to feast the villagers. That was many, many years ago, but Father still liked to tell how he got a chunk of meat from the hind leg. It was tough, Father always said, just tendon and gristle.

My brothers did not fulfill my parents' dream, so Father and Mother turned their eyes to me. Upon graduating from middle school, I applied to the high school affiliated with Shanghai Medical College, hoping that I could step from there directly through the gates of higher education. But out of the blue I was accepted by Shanghai Automotive School. I had never heard of it. I read an introductory description of the school the same day I received the admission notice. The truncated procedure reminded me of old-style, arranged marriages in which the groom doesn't know his bride until he lifts her veil.

Shanghai Automotive School was a technical school. It educated mechanics to repair automobiles. I thought it was fine. Medical school teaches you to repair people; automotive school teaches you to repair cars—not too much difference.

My parents were happy, too. They said I was much better off than my two brothers. So, on a fall morning in 1960, Mother readied a trunk of clothes and saw her youngest son down from the attic.

I was sixteen that year, the same age that Ling had been when he left home. At my departure Mother cried. In fact, Shanghai Automotive School was only in the western suburbs, and I could come home every weekend. I believe it was my age that reminded Mother of another of her sons, still far away in the remote territories.

When I first walked through the gates of the school, carrying my heavy trunk, I got the impression that it was a ranch. A huge expanse of grasses as high as my chin waved in unison. A Han dynasty poem had the refrain:

High, high the sky.
Wide, wide the land.
The wind blows the grasses
And the hidden buffalo are found.

But there were no buffalo in this grass. Instead, a few rusted-out trucks crouched among the weeds as if too busy grazing to acknowledge me. In less than one semester, however, my disappointment was totally replaced by awe.

Shanghai Automotive School had just been founded by the Shanghai Transportation Bureau. I was in the first class admitted to the school. In the late 1950s China began to produce trucks. Shanghai Automotive School was created to meet the pressing need for truck repair technicians.

When Shanghai was liberated, thousands of intellectuals were kicked out of academic institutions. They were shoved around with no place to go. Ultimately, many found havens on pushcart teams.

It was a blessing in disguise. By the time the Campaign for Freely Airing Your Views* started, the intellectuals had been out in the sun for seven or eight years. The sun had tanned away their pale intellectual appearances and burned out their intellectual complaints. With bent spines and lowered heads they pushed their carts all day, letting the wave of the Anti-Rightist Campaign wash over their backs. In 1960, when Shanghai Automotive School was created, some of those intellectuals who had crawled over the asphalt for ten years were summoned. They became my teachers.

At that time I only noticed that, even though their hands were rough, my teachers' knowledge was astonishingly pro-

---

* In 1957 Mao Zedong created the Campaign for Freely Airing Your Views, encouraging Chinese intellectuals to contribute suggestions to, and even criticize, the government and the Party. Many intellectuals responded. A few months later, the Anti-Rightist Campaign was launched. The intellectuals who had spoken out were labeled as rightists and punished.

found. The mystery of their origins was kept from their students for six years, until the Cultural Revolution began. Then with one shovel, all the dirty roots were dug up.

Mr. Ding, who taught solid geometry, had been the chairman of the Mathematics Department of the former St. John's University; Mr. Pong, who taught theoretical mechanics and principles of internal combustion engines, had been a researcher at the Nationalist's Chongqing Ammunition Research Institute; and Mrs. Zhou, who taught advanced Chinese, had been the cultural advisor to the former mayor of Shanghai.

During the Cultural Revolution there was an exhibition of remnants of the old society that had been gathered during house searches. A volume of Mrs. Zhou's poetry was included. The front cover had been crossed out with slashing brush strokes, but under the black ink a young woman still gracefully smiled.

Dr. Li, who spent his days fiddling with cotton swabs and bandages in the school's clinic, was a small weasel of a man. He liked to sit in the clinic and pick at his feet. I figured he must have been one of those dentists who pulled rotten teeth under their big umbrellas in the Penglai market. But one day I scraped my arm rather badly. Dr. Li held it and felt around the elbow joint.

"When you were five or six years old," he suddenly asked, "did you dislocate your elbow?"

I was amazed.

The same Cultural Revolution exhibition displayed a photo of Dr. Li. It was printed in a yellowing copy of the *Shanghai Daily,* dated 1945. Under the picture, the caption ran:

DR. KAIMING LI OF THE 19TH NATIONAL ARMY
IS TREATING JAPANESE POWs

The school's purpose was to educate intermediate technicians, but our overzealous teachers designed a different curriculum. We ignorant students had no choice; whatever they taught, we learned.

Ten years later, when I myself started to teach in the factory, I compared the material I had studied with the curriculum designed for a full-time college of technology. I got a real shock. In the four years of our intermediate technical school, we finished almost all the fundamental courses taught in the college program: advanced mathematics, analytical geometry, theoretical mechanics, material mechanics, thermodynamics, fuel chemistry, and on and on.

At the beginning of the Cultural Revolution, the students who had graduated in the first couple of classes were encouraged to return to the school and fight against the bourgeois intellectuals.

We did not quite understand the strategic purpose behind this unbelievable offer. To us, it was a sort of class reunion. It counted as working time and we got full pay from the factories that employed us. And it was a lot of fun, more than fun. We cranked out posters written in large characters, complaining of the mental tortures and poisonings inflicted on us by the bourgeois intellectuals during our four years of school.

We felt extremely influential and powerful. Whatever we wrote instantly became an accusation, a determination, a sentence. No evidence was needed; no witness was demanded. It was the first time in my life that I dared to condemn others freely, bearing no responsibility, fearing no consequences. I was thrilled.

Occasionally I was hit by a slight sense of guilt. I felt I was at a Live Fish Feast. Looking at the murmuring lips of the sacrifice, holding my chopsticks, I hesitated. But cheers rose, and an air raid of brushes was launched, splashing black ink. So I cheered, too, while I lunged at the prey.

On my posters I wrote how I had been overwhelmed by schoolwork. I said I had lost sleep, my heart raced, my eyes blurred, my ears rang, etc., etc. In fact, most of these symptoms could be traced to my early experiments in masturbation.

I remember the day that Mr. Pong lectured on a new generation of the rotary piston engine. He said that the reason rotary engines could not replace traditional, oscillating piston engines was that the temperature around the exhaust area of the combustion chamber was too high. Sitting in the class, I was struck by a brilliant idea. I believed I could solve the problem hindering the world's internal-combustion engine industry. After class I drew a sketchy diagram, put it in my exercise book, and handed it in.

A few days later the exercise book was returned, but my sketch was gone. I didn't pay much attention to it, figuring that Mr. Pong had probably thought it was a piece of scrap paper and tossed it out.

About two weeks later Mr. Pong called me into his office and asked me to sit across the desk from him. He swept the desktop clutter aside and spread out a sheet of No. 2 drafting paper. He said that he had drawn this diagram based on my sketch. Oh, my! I had never thought my doodle was so complicated.

Mr. Pong asked if the tri-view diagram accurately repre-
sented my original design. I examined it carefully and said yes.

"Okay. Imagine your design has been built as a prototype by
the Internal-Combustion Engine Research Institute. The exhaust valve is made of a manganese-titanium-nickel alloy.
Watch, I'll ignite your engine. The engine starts smoothly. Now
I start to accelerate. 500 rpm, 800, 1000, 1500, 2000. Notice the
flow of the exhaust gas!" Mr. Pong's fingers snaked along the
exhaust area on the chart, demonstrating the movement of the
gas. There was no way to analyze the flow on my sketch, but on
the tri-view diagram it was clear. The hot gas was compressed
into a narrow exhaust channel, rushing at the thin stems of the
exhaust valves. Suddenly I understood.

"Okay, okay! Stop accelerating!" I yelled. "The exhaust
valves are melting!"

A series of explosive pops came from Mr. Pong's mouth,
sounding exactly like the backfire from a tailpipe!

Mr. Pong, I said in one of my large-character posters, that
was you showing off your bourgeois intellectualism.

CHAPTER NINETEEN

Mr. Lu

Quite probably, the pervading bourgeois intellectualism of the automotive school was noticed by the authorities from the very beginning. They tolerated it simply because, I believe, the school was not solid enough to be picked on in its formative, "jelly" stage. But during my second year of study, new blood was infused into the teaching body. Mr. Lu was one of the "revolutionary intellectuals" cultivated by the new government.

Before the liberation, Mr. Lu's father had been a porter on Shanghai's docks. Belonging to the lowest economic class earned him the honor of being regarded as a "primary force of the revolution." After the automotive school was created, Old Lu worked there as a guard for more than a year.

Old Lu was an amiable person. When I carried my heavy trunk through the school's gate on my first day, a shout burst from the dark doorway of the gatehouse.

"Hold it!" Out came Old Lu. He loaded my trunk onto his handcart and trundled it to my dormitory.

In winter the unheated student dormitories were chilly. On cold evenings the students liked to crowd into the guardhouse to keep warm. There was a coal stove in the shack. According to school regulations, students weren't allowed to loiter in the guardhouse. But as long as we didn't make a big ruckus, Old Lu wouldn't kick us out. If he was in a good mood, he might even brag about his youthful days.

He told us how the freighters' hoists would lower a four-hundred-pound bale of cotton or tea onto his back. Old Lu said he carried the load down a narrow gangplank bouncing some thirty feet above the harbor's water.

"It was like an elephant walking a tightrope." Old Lu nodded his head and shook his head at the same time.

One evening he saw a student roasting an old bun on the coal stove. The bun was made half from corn flour and half from sorghum flour, and it was hard, black, and cracked. Old Lu sighed and began another story.

He said that one day during the Japanese occupation of Shanghai, he hauled a lady's piano. It was a hot day, and the lady invited him to take a bath in her apartment. As he was leaving, the lady gave him a flour sack filled with buns.

"One after another, this big, this big!" Old Lu gestured with both hands. "White! White as the woman's butt!"

"How did you figure that?" We grabbed him, shook him, trying to make him confess.

"I'll never tell." With a smile on his wrinkled face, Old Lu endured our torments.

As part of the political education program, the school asked Old Lu to address the student body, recalling and denouncing the sufferings of the old society. Old Lu even mentioned the heavy piano and the hot day. We all sat up, alert. With a barely detectable smirk, Old Lu smoothly omitted the white buns and the white butt from the speech that followed.

When Mr. Lu arrived at the school in my second year, his father was transferred elsewhere.

On his first day Mr. Lu entered the classroom, and all of the students began to snicker behind their hands—he had clearly been cast in the exact mold used to form Old Lu. Mr. Lu made no effort to hide his origin.

"Without me introducing myself, I'm sure you can tell that I am the son of Old Lu, the guard." He pointed out the window toward the gatehouse. "Right?"

The whole class burst out laughing. Mr. Lu laughed, too, his mouth stretching from ear to ear. From that first day we liked him. No wonder that lady was happy to give away a big sack of buns!

After graduating from middle school, Mr. Lu had been an apprentice in a garage. In less than half a year, he was sent to the Internal-Combustion Engine Department of Jiaotong University in Shanghai (China's equivalent of MIT). A three-year, intensive program there yielded a college diploma. Because our school urgently needed teachers, Mr. Lu spent his last semester shuttling between Jiaotong University and the automotive school. He studied and taught at the same time.

He was only around twenty then, not much older than we were. So after class was over, he often hung around and chatted with us.

"I feel like a panfried chestnut vendor. I sell my chestnuts as soon as they come out of the pan," he said. "Please excuse me if there are occasionally a few bad nuts in the bag."

We had no problem with him selling his chestnuts while they were still hot. The problem was that Mr. Lu was influenced by the bourgeois intellectuals and, without being aware of it, he began to imitate the old fogies' teaching styles.

Mr. Lu taught structural mechanics, which was a killer course. The stress equations necessary to analyze a single structure could easily fill half the blackboard. If you blurred your eyes, it looked like the millions of rivets on a steel bridge.

Bald Mr. Pong, who taught theoretical mechanics as if it was theatrical mechanics, regarded the classroom as his stage. We never saw him with a script. He didn't even bother to use chalk. He strode back and forth in front of the blackboard and recited formulas in dramatic tones that ranged from whispering to stentorian.

When he recited the equation for the even distribution of load, his voice was like the smooth flowing of a stream. But when he got to the equations dealing with shocking loads, the forces seemed to impact directly on his backbone. Explosive syllables shot out of his mouth. He panted, and his body jerked as he paced.

Just as our eyes told us at a glance that Mr. Lu was the son of Old Lu, our ears warned us immediately that Mr. Lu was imitating Mr. Pong's style. But he was not close enough to mastery to leave his script at home. He placed the mimeograph on the podium, trying very hard not to look at it.

As he paced, he clasped his hands behind his back, compressing his bulging triceps, looking like a handcuffed pirate. He closed his eyes and strode back and forth behind the podium as he painfully squeezed out the formulas. Every time he passed the podium, his eyes blinked like a spy camera, sneaking the next few lines from his notes. That was usually enough to keep him spouting for a few more minutes. But occasionally, when his ammunition ran out halfway through or his synapses misfired, he would suddenly open his eyes and point to an unlucky student.

"Pay attention. Pay attention!" he would shout. "No fooling around!"

In a classroom of fifty students, he didn't have to worry about finding a suitable scapegoat. While the whole class turned toward the condemned, Mr. Lu had a chance to reload.

Mr. Lu must have realized that his ad-libbing could lead him too far from the script. Before class ended, he usually distributed mimeographed pages of equations, pungent with fresh ink—more chestnuts just out of the pan. An announcement would be made: If the lecture differed from the mimeograph, follow the mimeograph; if the mimeograph differed from the textbook, follow the textbook. To this day, I still feel sorry for Mr. Lu. Since he had two sets of printed materials to follow, why was he so hard on himself?

Mr. Lu clearly sympathized with the hardships of learning. During exams, if a hasty student dropped a few tons of load out of the equation, Mr. Lu would only put a red exclamation mark on the paper. He might take a minor deduction, or none at all.

During my third year, Mr. Lu was promoted to academic dean, governing the educational affairs of the whole school. I was sure he would be able to handle his new position. Administration is different from teaching. You don't have to master a certain syllabus; tolerance and sympathy are the important

qualities. Less than two years after I graduated, on the eve of
the Cultural Revolution, Mr. Lu was appointed dean of the
school.

During the Cultural Revolution, students at the automotive
school formed a headquarters to direct their revolutionary activities on campus. The proletarians among the teachers, like
Mr. Lu, formed a teachers' headquarters. The two headquarters
joined forces to combat bourgeois intellectuals like Mr. Pong.

I didn't know if Mr. Lu's tolerance and sympathy could survive and function in that political climate. But as far as I can tell,
even though the old diehards at the automotive school were subjected to routine procedures like house searches, public parad-
ing, isolation, and verbal fighting, they did manage to avoid
bloody drama. It was one of the few exceptions in the educational community.

Skirmishes did occur, however, during the joint revolutionary operation between the two headquarters. Once, during a
celebratory get-together, the student commander suddenly condemned the teacher commander in front of the whole crowd.
He said that Comrade Lu, the dean of the school, was responsible for situations in which students from families of the Five
Black Categories were praised while students from families of
the Four Red Categories were ignored.* To his surprise, the
good-tempered dean of the school didn't buy it. Comrade Lu
swore a blue streak:

*The Five Black Categories were landlords, rich farmers, counter-
revolutionaries, convicts, and rightists; the Four Red Categories consisted
of workers, poor peasants, revolutionary soldiers, and revolutionary
officials.

"Fuck you, asshole! You damn piece of shit! How dare you say you're being ignored? You never study. You spend all your time trying to cheat! And you can't even cheat right! You've been caught red-handed several times. Everyone here is a witness, right?"

Cheers erupted!

"Liar! You're a damn liar!" the student commander shouted.

"Okay." With a smile, Mr. Lu cross-examined the defendant. "Just tell me one thing. How did you think of hiding crib notes in one of your socks? You thought it was a clever spy trick, but the lovely aroma alerted your teacher. Does everybody here still remember that dirty sock nailed beside the demerit notice?"

Hoots and catcalls!

"If it wasn't for me, the dean of the school, covering your ass all the time, who knows where the hell you would be kicked to, you stink egg!"

The student commander stood stunned by the blitz, his face red, his mouth agape, unable to say anything.

Mr. Lu realized he might have wounded his ally too deeply, so he tried to soften the blow. "Of course, for students, cheating is not such a big deal. To a certain extent, cheating is a kind of art, a kind of knowledge. When I was studying at Jiaotong University, if I hadn't cheated, how could I have gotten that damn diploma?"

Laughter burst forth from the room. Even the shell-shocked student commander scratched his head and chuckled.

CHAPTER TWENTY

The Pursuit of Oil

Maybe it was because we were studying automobiles and under-stood the importance of lubrication for engines. In our four years, the students' pursuit of oil reached frantic proportions.

When we entered school in 1960, our per-person monthly ration of cooking oil was eight ounces. By the time we gradu-ated in 1964, the ration had been reduced to four ounces. Pan-frying vegetables had long since been abandoned at the school. Boiling was the only method of cooking.

The vegetables were dumped into a pot of boiling water, given a few stirs, and scooped out. A spoonful of oil was driz-zled on top. That was it. The cooking water wasn't thrown away. A handful of salt, a scoopful of soy sauce, and a few drops of oil were added. The concoction was poured into a wooden barrel and carried to the center of the dining room.

"It's soup time!" the chef called.

Students rushed forward. Enamel bowls clattered.

The barrel was huge, and there was plenty of soup. The goal

126

of the students' haste was the oil. The oil that had been dropped in the hot soup and tumbled all the way into the dining room had dispersed into a floating membrane, reflecting an iridescent spectrum under the lights.

The manipulation of the soup ladle was the key to collecting the oil. Even if you were first in line and held the steel ladle, haste could be your undoing. If you plunged the ladle into the soup, the oil membrane would break and scatter.

Don't rush. Stay calm. Absorb the rush of students with your back. Hold your breath. Submerge the bowl of the ladle gently into the soup. Adjusting the angle of the handle, let the lip of the bowl parallel the surface of the liquid. Glide the bowl a quarter of an inch under the surface. Owing to the resistance created by the handle, the membrane will gather above the bowl.

The moment you choose to raise the ladle is critical. If you lift too early, the accumulation won't reach its maximum level. But you can't be greedy, either. When the membrane thickens and reaches the threshold of its surface tension, it will suddenly break and spread in all directions. Then you've lost everything.

No special instrument had yet been invented to measure the thickness of the oil membrane, but my naked eye was quite accurate. Although the color of the membrane changed constantly, there was a pattern that could be traced: red, orange, yellow, green, blue, purple; from red to purple, the length of the light waves decreases along the spectrum. This served as a sensitive indicator of the increasing thickness of the membrane. I discovered that the membrane usually broke around the time the color turned purple, and it was safe to lift up the bowl when the color was between green and blue. I succeeded almost every time.

Such a fat layer of oil floating in my bowl would mark me as a show-off. So on the way back to my seat, I would vigorously stir my soup with my chopsticks to break up the oil slick. In fuel chemistry this is called the particlization of the fuel. But oil is lighter than water, and the particles of oil could only hold their breaths under the liquid for a couple of seconds. Then they would rise, popping to the surface one by one, to form a new membrane. So as soon as I got back to my table, I poured the soup into my rice. The porous surface of the rice grains absorbed all the oil. With my treasure safely hidden, I was allowed to sit down and enjoy it at my leisure.

But there were some eagle-eyes in the room. Sometimes just as I was about to pour the broth into my rice, someone said:

"Hey! Would you mind sharing some of your soup?"

Damn! I knew the raptor's prey was not the soup, but the oil. But how could I refuse? I poured my soup into the bandit's bowl—it was a disaster! Before any broth could flow out of my bowl, the oil slid out in an avalanche! After a few painful losses, I developed an effective method for dealing with this shameless exploitation. If I had to give it a name, I would call it "Positioning the Oil Membrane by Air Current." It sounds very academic but wasn't too sophisticated in practice.

Put the guest's bowl between your bowl and your mouth. As you gradually tilt your bowl, gently emit a surreptitious zephyr from between your lips. The draft reaches the surface of your soup, applying a delicate pressure to the membrane of oil. The force of the pressure equals the downward gliding force of the oil, but in the opposite direction. The pure soup can flow out unhindered, while the oil membrane doesn't budge. The exploiter got a half-bowl of clear water, without a single particle of oil.

But I didn't want to be so stingy as to make people suspicious or angry. So when the sharing process was reaching its conclusion, I reduced the air pressure slightly, letting a few oil molecules separate from the mother body and flow away.

Finding the resource was important, but reducing usage could not be ignored. My skin was the major oil glutton and therefore the logical place to begin cutting corners. Even leather shoes, if left unoiled, will crack. My skin in those years was far from the tissue of a normal teenager. It was so dry and rough that every time I scratched, a flurry of white, dead flakes drifted down. My heels were cracked like tree bark. No oil came out of the fissures, only blood. Even my hair conscientiously reduced its consumption of grease. A plastic comb brought forth crackling static from the strands. Fortunately, there was no loose oil around, or I would have seriously worried about starting a fire.

CHAPTER TWENTY-ONE

Chopsticks

I always think chopsticks are an invention unique to Asian culture. Its historical and cognitive significance is no less than that of the Great Wall, the compass, gunpowder, and paper.

The greatest wisdom appears to be foolishness. Complexity ultimately ends in simplicity. Maybe it is because chopsticks are so simple that, just as air's weight was long ignored and white light was mislabeled as colorless, in thousands of years no one has ever scientifically or conscientiously researched them. A sensitive probe for examining the characteristics of Asian culture has been ignored. In my four years at the automotive school, I witnessed and experienced a splendid chopsticks civilization. I record it here for the benefit of future researchers.

In those days almost every male student carried an elongated pouch hanging from his belt. It was fashioned from canvas, leather, or leatherette. Like a warrior's dagger, it dangled all day from the student's waist.

Female students didn't wear belts, so the slim bags usually

hung from a cord around their necks. Their materials were more delicate: nylon, silk, or linen. Embroidery was often added as an embellishment.

Within these bags were chopsticks.

Because the rationed food offered insufficient calories, oxygen-intensive activities were not encouraged. Chess, card games, and calligraphy were the officially recommended pastimes. But the most popular activity was making chopsticks.

The number of students at the school increased each year, and new dormitories were constantly being built. Owing to limited funds, the dormitory roofs were constructed out of tar paper, straw, and bamboo. That bamboo became the primary source of chopstick lumber.

The selection of material was critical. Segments close to the plant's roots were too short. The meat between the skin and hollow core of the segments close to the top was too thin. A bamboo tree about one inch thick provided only a few middle segments that could be used to make quality chopsticks.

The bamboo poles were covered with a tarp and stored on the construction site. In the evenings, taking advantage of the absence of the construction workers, we started looting.

If only a few trees were missing, nobody would have noticed. But when an idea becomes a fad, things can easily get out of hand. There were hundreds of students. A newly delivered pile of bamboo would be half gone the morning after an all-out moonlit operation.

The superintendent of the construction site was furious and demanded that the student dormitories be searched. We got scared and threw our booty out the windows. The superintendent called a meeting of the school leaders to deal with the problem. He arrived with both arms laden with cut segments of bamboo. With a crash, he slammed the sticks down on the meeting table. The leaders, gathered around the table, looked like diners at an exotic feast.

The next day, a large notice was posted listing the price of the transgression: one bamboo tree = one big demerit. But the punishment was never really put into effect. After the immediate storm passed, the bamboo continued to go missing, but not in the same flagrant quantities.

After a bamboo segment was split open, it had to be dried in the shade for about a week. Experienced students put their bamboo strips on the mosquito netting over their beds. Their rising body heat helped evaporate the moisture.

Although the bamboo's skin is hard, it must be stripped away. If left on, the different densities of the inner and outer materials cause the chopsticks to warp. The best part comes from the quarter inch of meat just inside the skin. There the texture is even and dense, and the split will go precisely where the knife directs it.

The student-made chopsticks usually had a round cross-section. Round chopsticks require little skill to make. Wrap sandpaper around the strip of bamboo and sand for an hour or two, and a round cross-section is the result.

Only experts dared to make square cross-sectioned chopsticks. To make the four sides straight and symmetrical from tail to tip required real expertise. Sandpaper could not be used, because it would wear away the sharp edges you were trying to create.

To begin the procedure, you had to soak a fine-grained brick in water for a couple of days, and then grind it flat on a concrete floor. Laying the roughed-out chopstick on the brick, with one finger applying pressure to the tail and another to the top, you slowly ground the stick on the brick. Water was dripped on the brick to ensure fine grinding. Only by this painstaking process could chopsticks be formed with clear edges and smooth surfaces.

A boy student unprecedentedly produced a pair of five-sided chopsticks, which created a sensation on campus. The boy dedicated his efforts to a girl on whom he had a crush. Unfortunately, his gift was spurned and, desolate, he broke the chopsticks in front of his peers. This became the classic tragedy of the school year.

In addition to varying cross-sections, the top two or three inches were another place to show off your skill. The usual decoration was a few carved lines with inlaid color. Some students borrowed techniques from seal carving and sculpted miniature cats, turtles, and dragons out of the upper portions of the sticks. One student, who was good at calligraphy, carved two lines of a Song dynasty poem on his chopsticks:

"Vinegar fish from the West Lake," read one of them.
"Cinnamon meat from the East Hill," read the other.

He cherished the chopsticks as sacred objects, not intended for daily use. He employed them only on special occasions or festival days when excitement rippled through the student body:

"Today we are going to eat meat!"

Only then would he take his chopsticks from his trunk. Applying a thin layer of beeswax, he would polish them for at least ten minutes with a piece of suede. Then they were ready to be brought into the dining room.

Following the epochal five-sided masterpiece, chopsticks became a popular gift for boys to give to girls. If the girl liked the boy, she would accept his present and later give a gift to her admirer—a sleeve for chopsticks. The painstaking needlework expressed her sentimental attachment. We had never heard about Freud, but with our raw wisdom we subconsciously felt that there was some symbolic meaning, which could hardly be expressed in words, in this exchange, in the coming and going of the chopsticks and the sleeves. But school regulations clearly stated:

NO DATING ON CAMPUS

I think the regulation was well supported by science. Dating belonged to the category of oxygen-intensive activities. Before you could open your mouth, your heart started jumping and your cheeks were burning, clearly indicating a rapid consumption of valuable calories.

CHAPTER TWENTY-TWO

Sweet Potatoes

Students in the automotive school, male or female, received a rice ration of thirty pounds per month. Thinking of my father, who pulled a cart all day and got a ration of only twenty-nine pounds, I really could not complain.

Each student had a dining card. On the dining card was printed 4-6-6, or perhaps 4-7-5 or 5-6-5 or 3-8-5. The sum of each group was always sixteen. It meant sixteen ounces, or one pound. That was the weight of raw rice that each student was permitted to enjoy per day.

One pound per day was a constant, but how the pound of rice was divided into three meals was something every student could decide for himself. At the end of every month the student filled out a form and handed it in, selecting the next month's formula. This was a sacred right to determine one's own fate. The solemness of the students as they exercised their right was in no way less than that of the U.S. Congress when it decides the following year's budget.

If you applied cross-sectional research to the dining cards, you could probably make some significant psychological discoveries.

Female students may have had curvaceous figures, but they tended to have numbers with little fluctuation on their dining cards. Typical female plans were 4-6-6 or 5-6-5 or, the most popular, 5-5-6. They usually saved a one-ounce bun for late night nibbling under their mosquito netting. Every time I looked at one of those even-tempered dining cards, I could almost smell a trail of cheap perfume.

In contrast, most male students couldn't stand that kind of lukewarm regularity. Three meals a day, if divided too evenly, would bore the stomach. So they preferred to let their bellies enjoy the pleasures of expansion at least once a day. Their numbers therefore exhibited a certain degree of turbulence: 4-7-5 or 3-8-5 or 4-4-8 were typical male combinations.

Through longitudinal research on his or her dining card, you could measure the stability of a student's personality. Some students respected order and uniformity. Once decided, the combination would be adhered to in all seasons. Other students, in contrast, pursued variety and unrest. Their combinations changed every month. First they liked a fat breakfast and a thin dinner. A few weeks later they changed to a thin breakfast and a fat dinner. Sometimes, as soon as they had handed in their forms, they would pound on the superintendent's door exclaiming that they had a new inspiration. Change upon change, there was no tranquil time.

One night the boy who slept on the bunk below me was struck by a sudden whim. On his form he wrote 0-4-12. Obviously, he was going to gamble the store. To his great disappointment, the unprecedented plan was rejected. I believe it was the only case in school history in which the administration vetoed the free will of a student's stomach. If I were the Public Security Bureau, I would definitely have established a file on this particular student. His rejected, eccentric dining form, better than any inkblot test, undoubtedly predicted a future radical or extremist.

As I said, the figures on the dining card indicated the ration's weight in raw rice. If the dining hall served corn, pumpkin, or sweet potatoes, a conversion would be performed according to the Food Bureau's chart of equivalent calories per ounce.

A portrait of Chairman Mao hung on the east wall of the dining room. The portrait was huge—the light hanging from the ceiling could only manage to illuminate his crimson lips. Under his mouth was a quotation:

> I LIKE TO EAT SWEET POTATOES.
> I HOPE PEOPLE ALL OVER THE COUNTRY
> CAN EAT SOME.

Sweet potatoes did taste good. They were sweet. And a one-ounce equivalence of sweet potato was much bigger in volume than a one-ounce wheat bun. Three ounces of rice did not fill even your appendix, but a three-ounce equivalence of sweet potato would make your belly button pop out.

Of course, the joy of fullness created by the sweet potatoes was fleeting. A few gurgles and the sensation faded away. But at least your belly had an opportunity to stretch.

At the beginning of October, the sweet potatoes came to market. Truckload after truckload passed through the gates of the school. The slightly fermented, sweet fragrance drifted into the classroom, distracting even the eggheads from their books.

Sweet potatoes were cooked in a big bamboo steamer. The

cooked weight of a one-ounce equivalence of sweet potatoes was 5.3 ounces. It was weighed out on a scale for each student.

Sweet potatoes come in large and small sizes and the students unanimously preferred the large. Though mathematical talents differed greatly, every student understood that the bigger the tuber, the smaller the ratio between the skin and the meat. So every time the dining room served sweet potatoes, students stampeded the counters, trying to get the big ones.

The dining room superintendent asked the servers to give an appropriate compensation for small sweet potatoes. But "appropriate" is an elastic term, and a lot of arguments started about how to make "appropriate" appropriate.

The superintendent couldn't stand the disputes any longer. He approached Mr. Ding, who taught advanced mathematics, and asked him to figure out a scientifically appropriate compensation system. Mr. Ding gladly agreed. I was the student representative of the advanced mathematics course, so Mr. Ding let me join his research on the Sweet Potato Problem.

Mr. Ding and I went to the dining room to do field research. We climbed on the heap of sweet potatoes and dug around until we had collected a full basket of tubers of varying sizes and shapes. We brought them back to his office and examined them individually.

It wasn't difficult to measure the volume of each sweet potato. Just sink the tuber into a half-full measuring cup and read out a precise value from the increased height of the liquid. But the surface area was not so easy to deal with.

The down-to-earth tubers had not undergone any geometrical training. They had furrows and bumps, hills and valleys all over their bodies. Calculating the surface area of a single potato was enough to make a slide rule smoke. A sweet potato of a particular volume can be found in infinite shapes. Mr. Ding finally concluded that if we insisted on complete accuracy, the problem was unsolvable. So he designed a theoretical oval representative of the sweet potato population based on a variety of typical shapes and then established the function between the skin and the meat.

By then Mr. Ding was exhausted. He handed the problem to me and I drew a simple and concise chart following his formula. I duplicated several copies and pasted them inside the serving windows. On the chart, a 3-ounce potato was the standard. Potatoes smaller than 3 ounces moved down the chart in half-ounce steps—that is, 2.5 ounces, 2.0 ounces, 1.5, 1.0, and so on. Each was labeled with the appropriate weight of compensation. Tubers weighing more than 3 ounces moved upward on the chart in half-ounce steps and were accompanied by the appropriate deduction of serving weight.

The chart was so easy to understand and so simple to use that the servers were happy to have it. The problem was solved perfectly and the student stampedes never reoccurred.

The school praised Mr. Ding and admired his efforts to apply theoretical knowledge to practical life. Furthermore, he published an essay in the *Mathematical Quarterly*. The title of the essay was "The Surface Area of Irregular Objects." I was very proud that my name was listed at the end of the essay as the research assistant.

As a material reward, the dining room superintendent let us keep the whole basket of sweet potatoes. Mr. Ding and I split them fifty-fifty. I didn't dare to bring my share back to the dormitory. First, I had no way to cook them. Second, there were too many people around. So I asked Mr. Ding to take my share with him and ask his wife to boil one for me each day. Mr. Ding would wrap the cooked potato in newspaper and leave it on his desk. Every evening I would sneak into his office and take it. Then I would hide under my mosquito netting and quietly savor my reward. The boiled sweet potato was soft. Slowly I chewed and slowly I swallowed; nobody noticed.

Writing this, I feel it necessary to make a confession: that Mr. Ding and I used advanced mathematics to solve the SPP (Sweet Potato Problem) is not fact but fiction.

On the other hand, the inspiration for this fantasy was not fictional. One lunchtime I arrived at the dining hall a little late. I elbowed my way to the window. A few baby-mouse-sized sweet potatoes were tossed into my bowl. I protested until they added another tail.

I chewed the tough fibers and thought: There must be a way to solve the big sweet potato/small sweet potato dispute. But I had too much schoolwork already, and my enthusiasm for "saving the country through science" faded as sweet potatoes went out of season.

More than thirty years have passed. I have graduated from Middlebury College, and at the end of August I'm going to begin graduate studies at Tufts University. I have two months of vacation. I sit in a small country house in Vermont, recalling the past. Suddenly, the anguish and impulse I experienced in the Shanghai Automotive School is rekindled from the dead ashes, and I can't help but flesh out my youthful fantasy with details. I apologize if you feel you have been fooled.

CHAPTER TWENTY-THREE

Dentist Herb

Bao came home.

About two years after he left for the Steel Company of Gansu Province, he returned. He brought his copy of our family portrait with him. The portrait had been cropped—Bao had cut his own head off. He had felt confident that he could protect his brother, but he had eventually left Ling alone thousands of miles away.

The company had not trained Bao to be a steel analyst as the contract had promised; instead, he was assigned to break coal. For more than a year, Bao swung a hammer, smashing big chunks of coke and tossing the fragments onto a conveyer belt. Bao did not have a good temper. He quarreled with his bosses and blamed the company for its breach of contract. The company warned him that the Gansu Ore Mine needed workers; if he didn't watch his step he'd be reassigned there. The Gansu Ore Mine was a labor camp in the middle of the Gobi Desert.

Bao didn't want to be coal breaker all his life, and he didn't want to wind up in a labor camp, either. His only way out was to return to Shanghai. Bao tried to persuade Ling to come back with him. Ling tried to persuade Bao to obey orders. Ling said that the company was not in breach of his contract. He was studying to be an electrician and he liked it. He said that there was no legitimate reason for him to return to Shanghai.

Finally Ling agreed that it might be best for Bao to go home. Father and Mother were getting old, and the family needed a big brother to take the reins. So my two brothers put their apprentice stipends together and, stealthily, they bought a train ticket. On a winter evening in 1960, the wind blew from the Gobi Desert. Sand tinkled against the railroad tracks. Ling saw Bao off at the station. From that time on, each went his own way. One year later, Bao was in jail. Twenty years later, Ling was in the Party.

Since the liberation and the few brief years of prosperity that followed, food in China has been linked to residency permits. Being without a residency permit meant not having food. Although Bao, in desperation, managed to return to Shanghai, he was immediately faced with a serious supply problem. Because he could not get residency permission, he could not get a ration of food. In the years that followed, the five members of our family ate rations meant for four.

That year there was a plague of hepatitis, a result of the prevailing malnutrition. Many people swelled up like grapefruits, but no one in our family got sick. We managed quite well.

Mother became a live-in maid for a Party official's family on the other side of the Huangpu River. In addition to free room and board for her and my sister, Chuen, Mother could earn fifteen dollars a month. Mother used the money to buy high-priced sweet potatoes, corn, pumpkins, and squash from the peasants' free market. Every week, she let Bao carry a big bag home—all kinds of "secondary" food. At that time the government tolerated the existence of a free market, but rice, the "official grain," was strictly monopolized by the state and not allowed to be handled by private dealers.

After hours, when the official's family had gone to bed, Mother would often sit and knit long into the night. She made sweaters for other people. Each sweater earned her a ration coupon worth five pounds of rice—a semilegal transaction.

One midnight, Mother took the ferry across the river. On the dock a woman went into labor, and the people on the landing didn't know what to do. Mother knew midwifery, and she helped the woman into the booking office. After a few manipulations, she even managed to deliver the placenta. But she didn't dare cut the umbilical cord; she knew that operation was a risky one. She wrapped the baby and the placenta into one bundle and sent it with the woman to the hospital across the river.

A few months later the same woman, carrying her baby, bumped into my mother at the free market. She insisted on giving Mother ten dollars. Mother declined. Finally, the woman pulled Mother over to a quiet corner and slipped her a ten-pound rice coupon! Mother could not refuse that offer.

Father was pushing a cart for a living in those days. Each month he got a ration of only twenty-nine pounds of rice. If only every month was February! To power a pushcart loaded with a half-ton of freight for eight hours, each grain from Father's ration had to yield its maximum energy. Every morning, as he patted the rice into his lunch box, Father turned his back to us as if he was doing something shameful.

Father knew he couldn't save any food for his sons. So every Sunday in the spring, summer, and fall, he took Bao and me to the suburbs to collect wild vegetables. I was studying at the automotive school, and on weekends I always returned home to join the outing with Father and Bao. After a whole week's brain-wrenching study, collecting wild vegetables was a good time for me to relax.

In the fields of Shanghai's suburbs an herb called purslane, or "dentist herb," grew wild. In the old days there were many street dentists practicing in Shanghai. With a small table for his tools and a chair for the patient, he offered his all-weather service under a large umbrella. Like the rat poison commercials at the Penglai market, the dentists' advertising was graphic and effective—a blanket spread on the ground, displaying an assortment of the teeth he had collected from his clients. The tooth-like leaves of the purslane plants flourished in patches across the fields, looking like a fair of those grass-roots dentists.

We carried home burlap bags stuffed with dentist herb and dumped the plants into a large pot of water to boil for ten minutes or so. Then we spread them on the roof to dry. If the sun was strong, the green leaves would be dried to dark purple pellets by evening. Packed into bags, they would keep for months.

Preparing them for dinner was easy. Simply boil them until they softened and swelled; then stir in a cup of flour and the vegetable soup was ready. A little sweet, a little sour. It tasted good and filled the belly well.

Green hills and clear waters are traditionally linked with picturesque scenery. By those standards, the suburbs of Shanghai fall a little bit short. Shanghai lies on an alluvial plain, and there are no hills to enliven the distant view. Instead, the smokestacks of oil refineries and chemical fertilizer plants straddle the horizon. As if in compensation, black, yellow, and red smoke fuse into the blue sky, creating a water-color effect.

Yes, there are rivers. From a distance, they curve sinuously, resembling the brooks in classical Chinese paintings. When you get closer, however, you see a black ring of oil lining each bank, clearly recording the day's high tide.

But we had fun.

Bao was an expert at skipping stones. Launched from his hand, a broken piece of tile could skip all the way across the river and jump up the other bank, leaving a string of ripples expanding in the water. But occasionally there were failures. Once when he stretched his muscular arm back ready to shoot, he was distracted.

Two ducks were mating in the water.

The male was mounted on the female's back. Maybe the duck was worried about suffocating his girlfriend; he hastily paddled a few strokes in the water with his webbed feet, and everything was over. I was watching them, too, and did not pay any attention to my brother. Embarrassed that I might have noticed his prurient interest, Bao quickly tossed the tile he had been holding. It hit the water with a "plunk" and sank into the depths. No skips at all. It was as rushed as the duck had been.

A buffalo was tethered to a tree on the bank. He was relieving himself. The sight of a buffalo peeing was impressive. The splash of the thick column of fluid fully expressed freedom and decadence.

Peeing in the attic was a totally different experience. The chamber pot was thick and heavy. When I lifted it up, its weight seemed to impact directly on my groin, and it was a major effort to release the pressure. I preferred a kneeling position. With the pot on the floor, I was as careful as if I was adding sulfuric acid to a test tube in a chemistry lab. No rush, no splash. Any spill would inevitably create a yellow stain on the ceiling of our downstairs neighbor.

I envied the buffalo.

Father strictly forbade us to steal anything from the farm fields. Every time Father issued his warning, he looked at me. It seemed I was type-cast as a suspect. In normal circumstances I was trustworthy. But sometimes the tomatoes were too red to resist. So I dragged along behind Father and Bao, waiting for my chance. I suddenly shot out my hand like a lizard's tongue, and with a slight twist the fruit was mine. I never pulled on the plant. The shaking leaves would attract the attention of the peasants weeding in the distance, and I did not want that kind of trouble.

Bao knew my trick, but he remained quiet. When Father turned around unexpectedly, my brother would casually adjust his location, positioning himself between Father and me.

One bite of the newly picked fruit, and the sweet-sour juice, mingled with the green smell of the calyx, exploded in my face. I didn't forget Bao's collaboration. I would pass the remaining half, wrapped in a towel, to him. Bao solemnly accepted the bribe. Pretending to wipe his face with the towel, he stuffed the loot into his big mouth. No evidence was left.

But we were almost caught once. The sun was scorching that

day. Just as Bao tossed the towel back to me, Father called from a distance, "Give me the towel!"

Bao and I were stunned.

The pink flowers printed on the fabric might hide the blood of the slain tomato, but what about the smell? Father was no bloodhound, but it didn't take special training to identify the strong odor of the victim. No discussion was allowed. Grabbing the towel, I ran toward Father's shining head. As I passed a tall field of corn, I ducked between the stalks. I quickly dropped my pants and emptied my bladder on the towel.

CHAPTER TWENTY-FOUR

Bean Dregs Paste

As October passed, the dentist herb withered. It wouldn't sprout again until April of the next year. The stored-dried dentist herb could only suffice for a month or two. The rest of the food deficit had to be made up by other means, largely by bean dregs paste.

In those years, nearly everything edible required a food coupon. A bowl of noodles called for a three-ounce coupon. A bun with vegetable filling took a one-ounce coupon. A serving of wonton soup with only a few thin wrappers floating in the water required a half-ounce coupon. I believe that if a sparrow flying overheard pooped on your plate, you would probably be charged a few additional grams' worth of coupons—the sparrow had eaten grain, after all.

The only exception was bean dregs paste.

Bean dregs are what is left over after the oil is extracted from soybeans. They look like drained pulp and taste like shredded paper.

The menu board in front of the restaurant listed the price—ten cents per bowl. To advertise its unique selling point, there were four palm-sized characters above the price:

NO COUPON IS REQUIRED

The restaurant was only about a five-minute walk from our home. Its name was Full & Happy—if you are full, you are happy. The year-round disputes, arguments, and fights that took place in front of the restaurant provided a reverse proof of the truth posited by the name.

Bean dregs paste was served at eleven o'clock in the morning. On Sundays Father didn't work, I was home from school, and Bao didn't have a job to begin with, so we stayed in bed until eight o'clock. But by a quarter after eight we were already standing in line outside the Full & Happy. You might get your food if you were a little late, but the longer the bean dregs paste sat in the barrel, the more it expanded. The later you arrived, the lighter your bowl would be.

The line started forming long before the restaurant opened. The stove wasn't lit until nine. When the water in the cauldron boiled, a big barrel of bean dregs was dumped into it. The mixture was stirred constantly with a huge paddle that looked like the weapon of some ancient warrior. After a half-hour of boiling and stirring, enough wheat flour was added to make a paste. Around ten o'clock, the bean paste was scooped out of the cauldron and put in a wooden barrel wrapped in a padded-cotton blanket. The next hour was what I called the "postcooking expansion stage," in which the volume increased significantly.

A few tables stood in front of the restaurant. Those aged tables were the opposite of the oil-free food. If you were making soup, you could randomly slice a thin strip of wood from a table, drop it in the pot, and the broth would sparkle with grease. But we never sat at those tables to eat our food.

The Full & Happy was always punctual. At eleven o'clock, everyone sitting on the curb got to their feet. There was a spattering of buttock slapping. A cloud of dust rose from the line while the steam rose from the barrel.

"One bowl per person!" the attendant shouted. "Get your money ready. One bowl per person!"

One attendant served the paste; another took in the money. It went very quickly; in just a few minutes it was our turn. Our sequence in line had been decided in advance: Father was first, I was second, and Bao brought up the rear. The way we paid our money was also predetermined: Father held a ten-cent bill, which he handed to the attendant with his bowl. As soon as he got his paste he turned away. Bao and I always paid with a handful of one-cent coins and let the attendant count them one by one. Assume that it took the guy three seconds to count ten coins. Three seconds times two equals six seconds. Those six seconds were crucial if Father was to get a second bowl of paste.

Father was over sixty then. He was still healthy, but his running speed could no longer compete with younger legs. When Father got his first bowl of paste, he immediately ran toward the end of the line, where he would queue for a second bowl. The line was long, snaking along the sidewalk until it turned onto Temple of Letters Road. If it were not for his two sons stalling for six precious seconds, Father would have been passed by those behind us, greatly reducing his chances of getting a second helping.

Father ran awkwardly. He clutched his bowl with both

hands and managed to keep it level. Because he kept his eyes
fixed on the paste sloshing in his bowl, his neck muscles tightened. At the same time, his two legs had to produce maximum
speed. The rigid upper body and furious movement of his legs
created constant conflict. Father tried to stabilize his bowl by
stiffness, not realizing that his rigid, outstretched arms became
levers that transferred, or even magnified, the vibrations. So he
was forced to stop periodically and wait for the overflowing
paste to subside. Then off he dashed again.

When he finally reached the end of the line, Father had to
put his bowl down on the sidewalk. Placing his hands on his
knees, he bent over and fought to control his breathing. His
back heaved like a frog in a dried pond.

Bao and I usually reached the end of the line at the same time
as Father.

"Don't stop immediately," I urged Father as I gracefully
jogged in place, looking like I had just broken the world's record in the hundred-yard dash. "Keep moving. Keep moving."

Seeing Father's trembling calves, we knew he could not imitate me, so I let him take a break where he was, while we moved
along with the line. People usually honored Father's position in
the line when he slowly came to join us after catching his breath.

After the panting came the eating. We once brought an aluminum pot with us and poured the first bowl of paste into it.
The restaurant assistant caught us and strictly forbade our
"cheating." The bean paste was provided for immediate consumption. Pouring it into a pot created the possibility of profit-
able resale.

In ordinary situations Father could comfortably finish his
first bowl while waiting in line for the second round. The prob-

lem stemmed from the athletic activity. When he rejoined the line, Father's heart was still racing. The thin skin behind his ears revealed his throbbing pulse. But there was no time to wait. The first bowl had to be finished before we reached the restaurant again. Father ate while he was still puffing.

Bean dregs paste doesn't require much chewing—lift your chin and pour it down your throat. But you only have one throat to handle both food and air, and mistakes can happen at any time. When this occurred, Father would shove the bowl into my hands and cough to his lungs' content. The hairs of his beard stuck out like a porcupine's quills. His face turned as purple as a pig's liver.

If we were lucky enough to get a second helping, we would carry our full bowls as we slowly walked toward home. As we walked, we pretended that we were eating, in case the restaurant attendants were still watching us. The second bowls of paste were saved for Bao. My food at school was much better than my brother's, and Father didn't work on Sundays. It was a shame to consume food for no reason, Father said.

CHAPTER TWENTY-FIVE

Wet Dream

I had my first wet dream when I was sixteen.

Every fall there were always a few unusually hot days, "Tiger in heat" days we called them. I believe it was the heat that melted something long refrigerated in my body, or perhaps it was the accumulation of sin that called for a judgment. Anyway, it was the time for me to suffer.

It was a Sunday morning. As usual, Father, my brother Bao, and I queued up in front of the Full & Happy restaurant for a bowl of bean dregs paste. The line moved slowly down the sidewalk. We passed by a shoe repair stall; the repairman was fixing a sandal for a woman. The woman, sitting on a stool, rested her bare feet on a small rug.

Her feet were long and rounded. When the woman wiggled her toes, pink waves flickered under the translucent toenails. They looked just like the toes of the Bodhisattva.

"Hey, what the heck are you looking at?" Bao shoved me from behind. I found there was a space left in front of me. I had been in a trance for only a few seconds and quickly returned to deal with the food problem again. Those toes, however, did not let me escape. They attacked me that very night.

I dreamed that I was trapped between a pair of gigantic toes. I could not tell which two toes, because the flesh valley was so deep that I could not reach the top even when I stretched my arms.

Above my forehead I saw a ball of sweat seeping out from a pink wrinkle. The ball was expanding, getting bigger and bigger, while its color varied and ran like a soap bubble's. With a whoosh, the ball broke and splashed over my head. My arms were pinned by the walls of flesh and I could not wipe my face.

I inhaled; the smell was strange yet familiar. A little sweet, a little salty, sort of like overfermented rice wine with, perhaps, a baby's diaper among the rags that wrapped the fermentation barrel. I sniffed and sniffed, trying to recall the smell. But I felt dizzy, and my legs were weak. I was drunk. I was falling asleep.

Suddenly, with a jolt, I was alert again. I knew I was in great danger. I would be squeezed and steamed to a pulp if I could not get out of the trap.

I started to struggle. I wiggled like a worm. I managed to lift my right arm, and the gelatinous meat immediately replaced the space vacated by the limb, pressing even harder against my naked body.

I fumbled above my head, hoping to find something to grab onto. But those soft cliffs had no bushes at all. Finally, I felt a hole. I stuck my index finger deep into the pore, trying to anchor my body. A secretion oozed from the fissure. I tried to dig deeper into the hole, but my fingers slipped out. My body was sliding down when my toes caught in a crevice. I pushed against it, trying to propel myself upward, but my body did not rise. Instead, the foothold sank. I withdrew my toes, and the fat bounced back.

I was exhausted, and I knew I had no way out. I sensed my energy draining away. I felt the sticky walls that sucked at me start to rub and wiggle. It was the movement of a stomach digesting its food. And worse, from within my body, there came an answering pulsation, a response to the outside attack. It was a rebellion, a rebellion of the body against the will. I tried in vain to control the situation, but the vibration in my body accelerated ruthlessly.

Even worse, when the tissue withdrew, getting ready for another charge, my crotch shamelessly rushed forward, following the enemy. It was mutiny! It was the coup de grâce! I knew I had lost the battle. I gave up. I let go. I allowed the digestive juices to penetrate my skin. I let the slimy liquid erode my muscles. My body was expanding and disintegrating.

All of a sudden, I had a revelation. It must be a punishment from the Bodhisattva. But what sin had I committed? My mind was foggy. I could not recall; I could not confess. Well, since Lady Bodhisattva wanted me to go, I would simply go. Why should I ask why? Life was suffering; only death provided the way out. It was not easy to choose death, but once chosen, I felt a thrill of pleasure.

I began to moan. I moaned from the pain all over my body. I moaned from the pain penetrating my loosened muscle fibers. But the pain was a kind of willing pain, the kind of pain you would like to savor, to caress, to linger with. The pain gradually spread, losing its borders, losing its edges, diluting itself into a gray puddle of numbness.

My moan grew into a roar. I roared like a wounded lion.

Finally, all the flesh walls withdrew simultaneously and then launched the final assault. A howl was squeezed out of my throat. My body exploded.

CHAPTER TWENTY-SIX

Shovel-Shaped Fences

I've lost track of the number of curricula vitae I've filled out in my life. Those government-printed forms always had a box that asked:

> *Have any of your relatives ever been arrested, placed under sur-*
> *veillance, held in custody, reformed through labor, sentenced, or*
> *executed? State the date, the name of the relative, and the*
> *reason.*

Filling in my family's political status had already made me gloomy and answering that question depressed me more—two members of my family had to be put into that box.

Father's three-year surveillance came from his three-acre plot of land; the price was fair and had been paid in full. But my big brother's two years in custody was a messy account.

In my attempts to be honest and loyal to the Party in my school or factory, I asked Bao repeatedly for the reason he was incarcerated, but he never gave me a clear answer. What he said was that, shortly after he returned from the Steel Company of Gansu Province, one of his friends was arrested. The friend confessed that Bao had made some counterrevolutionary remarks. But Bao just couldn't recall what vicious comments he had made.

He was put in jail for two years and then released without sentencing, conviction, or explanation. It was as if he went somewhere for a vacation—he went and he came back, no special reason needed to be given.

But the box on the curriculum vitae still waited. My siblings and I put our heads together, convening our own grand jury, debating endlessly, trying to reach a verdict.

It wouldn't be a good idea to fill in "The reasons are unclear," because that would mean the problem had not been solved and Bao could be put back in jail for another two years at any time. Besides, the word "unclear" might imply that we thought the case was muddy and unjust.

Then just put down "Counterrevolutionary remarks"? Absolutely not. No verdict had ever been handed down; how could we assume the authority of the Public Security Bureau?

How about using "Further investigation is needed"? That was even worse. Bao had already been released; the case was history. Why stir up the embers of a dead fire?

Finally, we reached a consensus: "Ideological education." Ideological education was something everybody could enjoy. It even carried the implication of gratefulness on the part of the educated toward the educator.

Speaking of education, the windows of the jail of the Shanghai Public Security Bureau, Penglai District Division, looked just like the windows of a school. To prevent student distraction and keep passersby from peeking in, the local schools had built a wooden fence for each window that faced the street. The fences resembled the shovel blades of bulldozers. Air could pour in from the top, but the view was cut off.

Of course, the intensity of education is a little bit different in jail. Behind the wooden fences on the jail windows was another barrier—steel bars.

The Penglai District jail was a three-story brick building. The back of the jail faced the western end of Temple of Letters Road (the temple stood at the far end.) The road was narrow and damp with a high concrete wall that shadowed the pebble-paved street. On top of the wall broken glass glared, and barbed wire rusted above the shards. Rain draining from the flaking posts had dyed the moss on the wall a dingy brown.

A narrow black steel door was set in the bottom of the wall. I believe it was the back door of the jail. Beside the door stood a concrete garbage bin. The bin was flat and low, and jutted halfway into the street. Sunshine could barely reach the west end of the road, and the musty smell of garbage lingered throughout the year.

Because he had not been either officially accused or convicted, Bao's time behind bars was considered detention. According to the criminal laws of the People's Republic of China, no visitors are allowed during detention. According to the same laws, detention cannot exceed fifteen days. Of course, it was not necessary to inform us about the latter half of the regulation.

Bao had been summoned to the local police station, and he didn't come back. A few days later, the head of the block residents' committee told Mother to bring clothes, towels, and bed linens to the Police Office of Penglai District.

It was spring when Bao was taken. Later Mother brought summer clothes, and then winter clothes. With clothes for all four seasons, Bao settled down behind the bars. Since we were not allowed to visit, Mother started to shout.

I cannot remember exactly when Mother started to shout, but once she started, it became a routine. Every Sunday, Mother finished her employer's housework early. She crossed the river with my sister and came home.

When the clock struck six, Mother left the attic and walked toward the west end of Temple of Letters Road. Arriving at the back door of the jail, Mother stood across the street. Lifting her head, she gazed at the rows of windows with their shovel-shaped fences and began to shout. Since Bao's clothes had been delivered to the Police Office of Penglai District, her son must be held in that building. But Mother didn't know which floor, which room. So she always took a stance opposite the center of the building and aimed her shout at the middle floor:

"B-a-a-o-o! B-a-a-o-o!"

I rarely went with Mother. I was in automotive school then and understood the meaning of "political correctness" quite well. If one of my teachers or schoolmates caught me, I would be disgraced. And even worse, they might condemn me for "standing on the wrong side of the class struggle." So when I did occasionally go with Mother, I stood in the shade, keeping my distance from her. I would not shout, but only looked at the rows and rows of shovel-shaped fences, guessing which window hid my brother.

In addition to calling her son's name, Mother sometimes broadcast a tidbit of family news: Father just bought a pair of new tires for his pushcart; Little Chuen cut her braids; we installed a sink in the attic, and Father figured out how to use two whole bamboo trees as the drain pipe; Ling was doing well at the steel factory and would finish his apprenticeship in half a year. But there was never any response from the brick edifice, except for a few muted coughs.

On New Year's Eve of 1961, there was a big snowfall. It had been almost a year since Bao was taken.

As on previous New Year's Eves, Mother prepared a special dinner: steamed pork, red-cooked fish, sweet rice balls, red date cake, and white flour buns. The whole table was festively laden. As was our tradition on New Year's Eve, the entire family kow-towed in turn under the Bodhisattva's picture. The first bow was dedicated to Lady Bodhisattva; the second was for our an-cestors, thanking them for their protection during the past year and praying for next year's coverage. But unlike the previous years, we did not sit down to eat. Instead, we put on our hats, gloves, and scarves. Mother, Father, my sister, Chuen, and I, the four remaining members of our family, climbed down from the attic and walked toward the back door of the jail.

Every family was enjoying its New Year's dinner. The scents of wine and firecrackers mingled in the chilly air. Warm light spilled from fogged windows, etching a sequence of puffy or-ange holes into the immense block of darkness.

We tramped through the snow. Mother, holding Chuen's hand, strode in front. Father followed. I brought up the rear. We didn't say anything. The snow crunched beneath our feet. The streetlights stretched our shadows and then compressed them and then stretched them out again, but we felt no pain.

We stood in front of the concrete wall.

The broken glass that topped the wall was blanketed by

snow, a decoration befitting the holiday. The barbed wire trembled in the wind, shaking loose a few white flakes.

Toward those shovel-shaped fences Mother called:

"B-a-a-o-o! B-a-a-o-o!"

Toward those shovel-shaped fences Father called:

"B-a-a-o-o! B-a-a-o-o!"

Toward those shovel-shaped fences my sister called:

"B-a-a-o-o! B-a-a-o-o!"

And then, toward those shovel-shaped fences I called:

"B-a-a-o-o! B-a-a-o-o!"

After he was released, Bao said he never heard us calling him.

He had stayed only two nights in the Penglai District jail. Then he had been transferred to the Third Shanghai Prison in the western suburbs.

CHAPTER TWENTY-SEVEN

Bao Changed

Bao never spoke about his two years in jail. He didn't want to talk and we did not dare to ask, afraid of reopening the wound. But one thing was clear: Bao had changed.

When he was in middle school, Bao was friendly with the vendors in the Penglai market who sold Tiger Bone wine and Dog Hide poultices, the classic panaceas for sprains, bruises, and even arthritis.

To drum up business, the vendors would wrestle, spin stone barbells, and break bricks with their bare hands. Bao was an enthusiastic fan. Whatever they did, Bao would imitate. As a result, he received more than a few beatings from Father. But the bruises from Father's rod were well camouflaged by the bruises from the stone barbells, and Bao felt at ease.

He would often show off his newly learned skills to his two younger brothers. He'd take a wide-spread stance with hands on hips, then he'd tell Ling and me to each grab a leg and try to move it. He said his new feat was called "Buddha Rooted in

Earth," and even a crane could not budge him one inch from the ground.

Ling made an honest effort, and the ribs on his back wriggled like a pinned bug. I knew the straightforward approach was useless, so I plotted to ambush his Achilles' heel. I abruptly snaked out my right hand and attacked his crotch. With a yelp, Bao leapt into the air, and the hands on his hips lunged forward to protect the hitherto unguarded spot. His Maginot line was breached.

Bao had worked hard learning to break tiles. From a single tile he gradually advanced to breaking five at a time. Ling and I were assigned the duty of collecting the tiles. It was an awful job. The result of hours of painstaking scavenging would be smashed at Bao's single "Ya!" So I took a shortcut. I stole tiles from the construction site, and it ruined my reputation. Every time I passed by the fence, the elderly guard went on alert, craning his neck like a turtle in heat.

Despite our dedicated support, Bao did not master the premier stunt, called "Cracking a Rock Like an Egg."

"Now, ladies and gentlemen," facing the audience jostling around the white chalk circle, the performer announced the crowning feat, "I need a volunteer to pick a rock for me, and I'll show you something you won't believe. Anyone?"

"I'll do it!" A man from the crowd raced to the street corner to retrieve a cobblestone. With a single chop, the performer smashed the stone with his naked hand. Cheers burst from the audience. Then the broken pieces were passed through the crowd for closer examination. People were astonished and admiring.

We were disappointed that Bao could not match the masters.

Finally Bao divulged one of his friends' secrets. Bao told me that "Cracking a Rock Like an Egg" was a scam, that the guy picking the rock was a shill. The cobblestone had already been broken with a hammer and then glued back together with sticky rice. Wax had been rubbed over it to hide the cracks. When dried, the sticky rice sparkled exactly like the granite crystals.

The performers may have cheated while cracking rocks, but playing with the stone barbells was a real feat. To get the hundred-pound weight dancing over bulging muscles required many years of dedicated practice.

Although Bao's skills were a far cry from the professionals', two chunks of muscle proudly bulged out of his chest. Almost every day he asked his two brothers to feel them.

When he got out of jail, however, his pectorals had disappeared. Maybe they hadn't really disappeared, but had melted like two lumps of sheep fat, flowing down along the emaciated rib cage and ballooning out his belly. But he never asked us to feel his protruding paunch.

Bao had been a champion fighter. I remember once Bao took us to a swimming pool. He was about fifteen. Ignoring the repeated commands of the lifeguard, my brothers and I kept roughhousing in the water. The lifeguard got angry and dragged Bao out of the water and onto the deck. Without any warning, Bao swiveled at the waist and landed a heavy blow to the lifeguard's stomach. The guy doubled over, clutching his belly and moaning. Fortunately, Bao's back had been scraped raw when he was dragged out of the pool, so it was a fair trade. Both sides were even. We were kicked out of the pool and that was that.

Bao taught us to fight.

"The most important skill," he instructed his two apprentices, "is being desperate."

Bao's doctrine became my motto. No matter how you swear, I can ignore it, but hands off, please. Along with my increasing age and a growing understanding of my status in society, my spirit of desperation decreased. But the decline was much more dramatic in Bao's case.

One day Bao and I were out collecting wild vegetables. It was two years after he had been released from jail. On the way home, each of us carried a big sack of dentist herb. It was rush hour, and the ferry was overcrowded. I had pushed Bao onto the boat, but I was still jammed outside the steel gate. Unable to squeeze forward, I deliberately blocked the gate from closing. I knew that as long as the gate remained open, the boat couldn't leave. The crewman was furious and slapped me. I dropped my bag and jumped the guy. It was too crowded; my charge failed. The gate closed with a clang. Standing on the edge of the dock, watching the ferry slowly pull away, I shouted:

"Get him, Bao! He beat me!"

To my great shame, I saw that, on the stern of the boat, the crewman was yelling and swearing at my brother. Standing by the railing, Bao bent his head, let his arms hang and his mouth fall half open. He looked like an idiot.

Bao had been full of energy; he could hardly sit still. Even at night, when he was sleeping, it seemed he was still playing with the stone barbells. He rolled from one end of the pallet to the other. Sometimes Father got in the way, so he would roll all the way back, running over his two brothers, making them squeak like mice. But after our two-year separation, Bao turned into a Buddha.

He would sit on a wooden soapbox and remain frozen for hours. I thought that it might be the beam above his head that was holding him down, so I moved the soapbox into the middle of the attic. But Bao still bent over, hands on knees. Half-asleep, his eyes remained fixed on the floor two feet in front of him. The sun coming in through the window silently moved his shadow across the floor from left to right. Then like a piece of paper folded at the waist, the shadow was pasted on the east wall. Sometimes a fly would land on one of his ears. Maybe there wasn't much blood left under the skin; after meandering around for a little while, it grew bored and flew away.

When he got out of jail, Bao had two nasty sores on his buttocks. Mother asked for leave from her job and stayed home to clean his sores and change the dressings every day. If I was at home, I would be Mother's assistant. She worked with a feather-light touch, afraid to hurt her son. But Bao's pale pelvis stuck out as if cast in plaster, seemingly without any feeling.

After dinner Bao would slide onto his pallet and fall asleep. Every night he ground his teeth loudly. Except for that, he lay there as quietly as a weathered rock. Facing the wall, with legs curled up, he wrapped himself in a blanket. The folds in the blanket remained unchanged from evening right into the next morning.

Bao used to eat like a firefighter. Before Mother and Father could sit down, he had already wiped his mouth and gone running down the stairs. But after he came home from jail, his eating habits changed entirely.

He would send a half spoonful of rice into his mouth. Slowly he chewed and chewed. Curious, I put down my chopsticks, and watched to see in what century he would finish abusing his spoonful of rice. Noticing that I was watching, he closed his eyes and let his jaw muscles continue their masticating. I had to quit—my eyes grew tired.

The way he held his bowl was strange, too. He rested his left arm on the table, curved into a semicircle, protecting his bowl like a harbor. If any rice fell from the table, he had to bend down to pick it up, but his left arm remained in its defensive posture. The twisting of his body made him pant. As he panted, he stuck out his tongue to lick the dust off the grain of rice. Then he sent the rice to his mouth—another decade of grinding.

Although Mother never allowed us to leave a grain of rice in our bowls, she never permitted us to lick the bowls, either. But in front of all our eyes, Bao gracefully polished his bowl with his tongue. The bowl, covering his face, revolved slowly. The tip of his tongue flicked over the rim, like a snake peeking from behind a boulder. After licking, he put his bowl down on the table and, blankly, looked at Mother as she wept. For a long time after he got out of jail, he didn't allow anybody to wash his bowl. It didn't look as if it needed washing, anyway.

CHAPTER TWENTY-EIGHT

The Sadness of the Phoenix Fish

I don't know whether I read it somewhere or heard it from somebody, but some mountain villages in ancient Japan had a custom called "carry the old on your back." When the elderly reached a certain age and could not work anymore, they would be carried on the back of their son or grandson into the mountains. The ancestor would be put down in a quiet place. Sitting cross-legged, forsaking food and water, the elderly person would peacefully fade away.

I often think that if this archaic practice from the island country became as popular in twentieth-century Shanghai as Sony color TVs, many of the social problems plaguing China's largest city would be solved in no time.

Unfortunately, Shanghai lies on an alluvial plain and its highest mountain is Red Hill in People's Park. A ten-foot-high crimson pavilion sits on the peak, its pinnacle reaching the vast altitude of twenty-five feet above sea level. Courting couples have a hard time squeezing their rear ends into the packed pavilion or even onto the stone steps leading to the summit. If you did manage to trample over people's feet and carry your father to the peak, it would still be inconvenient to put him down on those clustered heads.

Father had been a large man. When we moved into the attic, he had stood in the center of the room and been forced to bend his head to avoid the highest beam. But not long before he died, no matter how he stretched out his arm, he could not touch the flour tin hanging from the ceiling.

In fact, Father's back began to stoop right after he turned sixty. He was still pushing a cart then. Cart pushing requires that you bend your back, so Father didn't pay much attention to his deforming spine.

One day, when he was sixty-nine, he was working with his partner, pushing a heavy load of cement up a bridge. As usual, Father was pushing hard on the back of the cart. When a cart reaches the top of a bridge, usually the pusher straightens up his back and jogs along as the lead man steers the cart downhill in a graceful glide. But this time Father couldn't straighten his back. The cart took off downhill and Father fell forward, bruising half his face.

Father assumed that the curvature of his back was a result of the weakening of his *yang,* or male, energy. "Buffalo Whips," or dried buffalo penis, is the special remedy for strengthening the *yang.* But a whole week's earnings from pushing a cart was hardly enough to buy a dose of the tonic. Just as he had figured out how to use bamboo trees as drain pipes, Father ingeniously devised an alternative remedy. On Sunday mornings Father took a basket to the market and searched among the meat booths. He collected loads and loads of the same organ from pigs. He boiled them in a pot until the entire attic reeked.

A teaching from the sutras of Buddhism says, "Believe it and it will work." Father's case, however, was a rare exception. Although he deeply believed the pots and pots of pig "whips" could strengthen his back as steel bars reenforce concrete, he forgot a simple fact: the pigs had all been castrated when they were piglets. The male organs remained; the male energy had long been cut off.

Stubbornly, Father continued to eat them until he reached seventy-two, but nothing happened to his back. His pushcart colleague lost confidence in his back before he did, and no one dared to risk working with him anymore. So Father had to say good-bye to his cart. He secluded himself in the attic and remained a hermit for the rest of his life.

The year Father quit his business, the attic's population fell to a historic low—Bao married and moved out; my sister, Chuen, settled on a farm in Yunnan. So the attic held only Father, Mother, and me. I had already graduated from the automotive school and returned to the attic. Every day, I went to work in the morning and came home in the evening. I worked in a truck repair factory.

The pushcart business paid on a daily basis; there were no health benefits and no retirement plan. Perhaps because Father no longer had to jostle his way through the streets, the white fog of his cataracts had the chance to settle in and obscure most of his sight. Then Father could do virtually nothing but eat.

Mother was still healthy. Although she was no longer able to work as a live-in maid, she could still sew at home, and she began to take in tailoring work. Her sewing style was not fashionable, but her handiwork was solid, with no shortcuts. And it was cheap. So she had a steady supply of customers.

My brothers and I each contributed five dollars to Father every month. Even my sister, Chuen, would sometimes send a few dollars back from faraway Yunnan. Every time she received money from her daughter, Mother faced the sky outside the southern window and yelled: "You little witch, are you trying to kill yourself? Who the hell needs your money here?" Then she cried.

From an economic point of view there was no need to carry my father to the mountains yet. But Father did not notice that his youngest boy had quietly grown up. I no longer slept soundly by his big feet.

Among the reefs in tropical seas live the phoenix fish. Their courting rituals are elaborate. The male fish begins by performing a complex dance around the female. If the lady fish is impressed by her suitor's gyrations, she inspects the candidate's hunting ability. The male outdoes himself, catching shrimp and tiny crabs to bring to his ladylove. After a good meal, the bloated female waggles her way into the male's nest, inspecting the dwelling conditions. Even if the male is a perfect knight, if his home does not come up to scratch he still risks losing his prospective mate.

I was twenty or so. I had already inherited Father's preshrinkage height and his straight-until-death nose. If I graded my own male charm, I would give myself a B or B+. As for my ability to earn a living, I had graduated from technical school and my position as a technician's trainee put me well above the average. So a few girls reached the final stages of courtship with me.

"We've known each other a couple of months," the shy girl would finally launch the attack. "Don't you think it's time for me to meet your parents?"

I knew with complete certainty that the blushing girl was not interested in paying her respects to my parents. She wanted to inspect my nest—damn it!

To my great regret, after a visit the girls dove from the attic, swam back into the sea of females, and never returned.

Mother did her best to help. Before each prospective daughter-in-law's visit, she mopped the floor until it gleamed like a boat's inside cabin. Mother dressed Father in clean clothes. She soaked Father's big hands in warm water to soften his turtle-shell–like fingernails and trimmed them with her sewing scissors. Mother then washed her hair and arranged it into a bun. She looked majestic.

Father could not see anything, but he knew a distinguished guest was visiting. He sat on his stool and stared forward, the window panes reflected perfectly in his white corneas.

Mother had washed all the chopsticks and dishes with soap. A special meal was prepared: panfried eggs, red-cooked fish; even the bok choy gleamed with oil.

The girl ate with extreme delicacy. Her mouth was so tiny that a half grain of rice had a difficult time squeezing through. While eating the girl looked around; then she asked my parents in a soft voice:

"By the way, do you live downstairs?"

"Oh, no," hastily, Mother answered. "My husband and I sleep on the other side of the attic. Long-long sleeps on this side."

Mother told a fib, moving Father to the southern pallet ahead of schedule. It seemed that the northern side of the attic was already her new daughter-in-law's territory.

"I like this attic very much," noticing the girl's disappointment, Mother murmured placatingly. "In winter the whole room is filled with sunshine. In summer the breezes blow from everywhere. You don't have to go downstairs to air out your bedding. With the door closed, you have complete privacy. To be honest, we're old. How many years do we have left?"

As she spoke, a disturbance suddenly arose from where Father sat. Knowing something was wrong, Mother interrupted her monologue, rushed to her husband's side, and dragged Father to his feet. I had already dropped my chopsticks and handed the chamber pot to Mother. Mother positioned herself between Father and the girl and said:

"It's nothing, nothing. Eat, eat . . ."

Awkward silence.

Father peed.

My heart ached from the tinkling sound.

CHAPTER TWENTY-NINE

Travel Pass and Wheat Flour

I lifted the trapdoor and climbed up to the attic. Once again I saw Father jammed in the corner, his head wedged between the ceiling and the floor.

It had happened a couple of times before I understood the strange situation. Father would manage to crawl into the corner, but because of his bulky proportions and his rusty joints he could not crawl backward, let alone turn around in the sharp point. So he stuck there, like a stranded whale.

But Father, composed as usual, did not bother to struggle. He lay on his back with his arms relaxed. A pair of bare feet, huge and cracked, like eroded tombstones, jutted out toward the edge of the trapdoor. Father knew that his son would come to his rescue again.

It was quiet in the attic. Dust particles hovered in the beams of the setting sun, hinting at the chaos of a few minutes ago.

I was not in a hurry. I poured out a cup of water from the thermos. I took a sip. It was too hot, and I put down the mug.

Issuing a sigh, I stood up and began to rescue my Father. I grabbed his feet and, with all my strength, dragged him out of the corner. Father trusted his son completely; he just let me do the job. During the whole process he did not move even a single toe.

At last Father was out of the corner, but he still lay on the floor. Only his eyelids twitched slightly under the sun's rays. I spaded my hands under the back of his neck and lifted him up. I pushed a stool under his rear end. Finally Father sat, while I stood panting. With his eyes still closed, Father obediently let me brush the dust from his head with a towel. He looked like a jar just taken out from storage. The dust got in my nose, and I sneezed and sneezed.

"Quit messing around; quit your stupid searching, okay?" I bent over and shouted at his skull. "I told you, the police took it, took it long ago. Do you hear me?"

It was obvious that there were no auditory nerves on his glossy scalp, which bounced back the sound waves with hardly any loss. My own eardrums were the only victims of my angry voice. I knew no matter how loudly I shouted, tomorrow, or the day after tomorrow, Father would do it again, making another search, another mess, and wind up stuck in that corner again.

Father died at eighty. In the last few years of his life, all of a sudden, he wanted to go home, the home thousands of miles away, a small village beside Poyang Lake in Jiangxi Province.

Sometimes on Sundays Bao brought his infant daughter to the attic. Bao's recovery had taken several years. Finally he found a seasonal job in a foundry, cleaning sand from iron castings. And he married. His wife was unusually quiet, probably the result of an accidental electric shock she had suffered as a little girl. But their baby daughter was a chirping bird. Holding her first granddaughter, Mother was so happy that she rocked her chair until all the bamboo joints squeaked merrily.

Father, however, was totally preoccupied with his own monologue. His granddaughter reached out a tiny hand to grab his beard, but Father kept on uninterrupted, continuing his murmuring. Sometimes in the midst of his mumbling, he dug his fingers into his mouth and picked out a loosened tooth. Then the soliloquy continued in a slushier voice.

I tried very hard to understand the content. But there was no need to worry if you did not catch it at the first hearing. Like the news from the BBC, every thirty minutes or so the broadcast would repeat. Finally, I got Father's story.

Father said Poyang Lake had fish in abundance, and his father had been a good fisherman. Father said my grandfather liked catching fish in the winter but never used a net. He said the catfish were as fat as cats and preferred being warm just as cats do. The catfish liked to dig holes in the bank under the water. Sometimes scores or even hundreds of catfish packed themselves into a single cave to keep warm. My grandfather often brought my father in a boat and rowed slowly along the bank. Grandfather could locate the fish cave by the air bubbles rising to the water's surface. He then took off his clothes, gulped a few mouthfuls of a potato liquor, leaped off the boat, and dove deep into the water. Fish were flung on board, one after another.

Father said catfish jelly was delicious. The catfish were boiled in a big pot, and then the pot was put out in the snow. By the next morning the jelly was ready. You had to be careful not to drop your spoon on the jelly, or it might bounce back and hit your nose.

Father said Poyang Lake had robbers in abundance as well. His father always kept an ancient blunderbuss in the bedroom, and he always kept one incense stick burning all night long— so he could touch off the gun at any time. But one day my grandmother finally discovered that her husband had never loaded gunpowder into the muzzle. She was furious, accusing her husband of not being serious about protecting her and their family.

"Do you really want me to fire the gun when pirates break in?" my grandfather argued. "Let me tell you what would happen. Bang! A big smoke—like a firecracker! But I doubt this piece of junk could really knock anybody off. One thing I do know is that the whole family would then be chopped into mincemeat."

"Then why do you keep incense burning every night?" my grandmother asked.

"To make you sleep well," her husband answered.

But eventually, one midnight, brigands did raid the village. My grandfather grabbed his wife and son and jumped out the window. My grandmother held my father down in the pond behind the house, allowing only his mouth to remain above the water. After the bandits left, the boy climbed out of the pond and felt something wriggling at his crotch. His mother put her hand into his pants, and her face turned pale.

"Don't move," she told him. "The snake will bite if you move."

My grandfather crawled out of a haystack and pulled an eel from his son's trousers. It was three feet long.

Father said when he was a boy, he never used tissue to wipe himself. Tissue was expensive and was used only to kindle pipes. The tissue was rolled up tightly to form a stick of kindling. The lighter was two pieces of flint. The sparks from the flint hit the "hot cap," or charred top, of the tissue rod at the same time that air blown from the smoker's lips reached the sparks. Flame rose from the kindling.

The hot cap was essential for ignition. After the pipe was smoked, the kindling was always carefully put back in a reed tube wrapped with silk thread and carried on the smoker's belt.

One day my father accidentally broke the hot cap off grandfather's kindling. Grandfather was very upset. That day they were planning to watch the annual dragon-boat race on the lake. Grandfather canceled the family outing because the hot cap was broken. It was a bad omen.

"Yes!" A smirk elbowed its way out of Father's tangled wrinkles. "I'll bring a lighter back to my father. A real lighter!"

Once I became so curious that I could not help interrupting Father's memoirs.

"If you did not use tissue," I asked, "then what did you use to wipe yourself?"

"Bamboo chips." Father did not look at me; his opaque eyes gazed at nothing.

After my interruption that day, every time Father reached the episode of the canceled trip to the dragon-boat race, he would always pause for a few seconds, waiting for my former question. Then, with his eyes still gazing at nothing, he answered:

"Bamboo chips."

Father also mentioned his ex-wife, a totally alien concept to me. Father was planning to bring her a gift. He said he had not heard anything from her since he divorced her.

"A few yards of print fabric will be nice. She likes silk, white silk with pink flowers. But I think linen is more substantial," Father muttered. "Well, maybe silk is okay, but definitely not that kind of gaudy Japanese junk!"

I was surprised that Father remembered those anecdotes from more than seventy years ago in such vivid detail. In his mumbling, however, Father never mentioned anything that had happened since we moved to Shanghai. Perhaps the last twenty-five years of his life had not fully fermented, and they were not tasty enough to ruminate about yet.

Father not only murmured; he acted.

Every time that he was left at home alone, Father searched around, making a big mess. His eyes were almost completely obscured by cataracts by then. So searching around really meant pawing around, sniffing around. He grabbed a piece of paper, first rubbing it with his fingers, then sniffing it with his nose—but it was not what he wanted. He tossed it away and continued his frantic hunt.

Father was searching for a travel pass.

When Father left his hometown with our family, the Land Revolution had begun. The current target of the Red Peasants Association (RPA) was the big landlords, and Father's three acres of rocky fields had not yet aroused any attention. Father asked the RPA for permission to visit his father-in-law in Hunan Province. The RPA inspected our house; everything was still there. The RPA inspected our simple luggage and found nothing valuable. So a travel pass was issued. I was five years old.

We left early in the morning. We had a dog. I vaguely remember his name was Wet something, Wet Nose perhaps. Wet Nose was sleeping beside the stove that morning. The charcoal in the stove was still glowing. Comforters for the bed were folded neatly beside the pillows. We would be back when it got dark, I thought. Wet Nose did not even run to the door to wag good-bye to us. When it got dark, we would return, Wet Nose must have thought, too. The chairman of the RPA asked Father to buy a few packs of Camel pipe tobacco for him. When we arrived in Hunan, Father mailed two pouches of tobacco to the chairman, but he himself never went back.

I saw that travel pass when I was around six. It was a piece of rough straw paper with brush writing. I could not read the characters then, but I remember there was a huge, square seal with a star in the center. Oil from the red ink had penetrated the straw fibers, which had not been entirely pulped.

That piece of straw paper was amazing. Not only did it enable us to pass all the checkpoints on our way out of the province, but it also allowed Father to stay in Shanghai for the rest of his life. He was only sentenced to three years' surveillance instead of being sent back to the village as an escaped landlord. We did not know what would have happened to us if we had been sent back. But we did know that Jiangxi Province, the original base of the Red Army, was very enthusiastic about the Land Revolution.

"Revolution," Chairman Mao said, "is not as polite as a dinner with your friends."

In Father's hometown, most of the landlords perished shortly after we left. Father was probably the only one who continued to live for a couple of decades and finally reached his eightieth year of age—fifteen years longer than the average life span in China! Very little was known about the fate of those landlords' families, but judging by the sparse and fragmented information we received, I believe that I am a rare exception, who crossed the border of the county, crossed the border of the province, and finally crossed the border of the country and reached the United States.

All of this came from that piece of straw paper.

One day at school, we were reading a story. I remember the title: *A Shepherd Boy Caught an Escaping Landlord.* The whole class looked at me.

When I got home I asked Father to give me the travel pass. I wanted to show it to the class. I wanted to tell them, "Yes, my Father was a landlord, but he was not an escaped one." To my great disappointment, however, Father told me that the police had taken the travel pass. I imagine it is still kept in Father's file somewhere in a damp basement of the police station.

But all of a sudden, Father started to search for it in the attic.

"I'll bring the pass back and show it to the RPA," Father said. "They permitted us to leave; they would surely permit us to come back as well."

Going back home meant traveling thousands of miles. Food had to be prepared. The best food for travel, according to Father's experience, was panfried wheat flour, the traditional meal on our family's outings. Dry and compact, it was easy to carry. Soldiers toiling in the civil war usually put the flour into sausage-shaped pouches, and wrapped them around their waists, beneath bullets and grenades.

Virtually no flour could survive at home. No matter where you hid it, within a few days, Father would find it and fry it. Though Father could no longer judge the flour's doneness by the change in color, his sense of smell remained intact. When the sweet smoke circled in the attic, Father lifted up the pan, and fumbled his way to the table. Knocking over a few bottles or jars or cups, he put the pan on the table, and waited for it to cool. Then he packed the flour in a one-gallon tin. His palm, armored with thick calluses, slammed the lid again and again. The lightbulb hanging from the ceiling shook as if it had malaria.

Nobody was allowed to touch his stored-up provisions. Worrying that the flour might spoil, Mother once sneakily pried one of the lids open. But before she could slip any flour out of the tin, Father caught the smell.

"Eat, eat, you pig!" he slapped his lap and shouted. "What will be left for the trip if all the food is eaten?"

He stood up with both arms stretched forward like twin rockets ready to fire. He staggered toward the source of the smell, paying no attention to the bumping of his head against the beams.

"Okay, okay!" Mother was scared. "I won't touch it, I won't . . ."

Father had a large collection of tins. When he was working as a cart pusher, he picked up an empty paint can now and then. He would put the can on the roof and light a crumpled newspaper. He tossed the burning paper into the can. The sooty smoke from the burning paint remnants engulfed the airplanes passing overhead. When the smoke finally dissipated, Father furiously rubbed the tin with a dampened rag dipped in coal ashes until the metal was exposed. He applied tung oil to the inside and outside of the tin and let it dry for a couple of days in the sun. Then the container was ready to use.

But the can manufacturers never expected their product to undergo that kind of rough treatment. After being burned in the fire and rubbed with ashes, the original seal was long gone.

When the rainy season came, moisture got into the recycled tins. The flour grew moldy and expanded, popping open the lids. Numerous tiny bugs flew out from the tins and circled around Father's bald head.

Father did not panic. He refried the bug-infested flour, one tin after another, and then packed the perfect mixture of plant protein and animal protein back into the tins for yet another storage cycle.

CHAPTER THIRTY

Cricoid Cartilage

It was a Sunday afternoon. Father was dozing off.

The sun cast the shadow of the window panels on his body; it looked like a torn fishing net tangled on a stump.

Father sat in a chair, cushioned by an old sheepskin. His feet were buried in a rattan basket stuffed with rags. The basket was used for cooking rice. When the boiled rice was half done, we removed the pan from the stove, put it into the basket, and covered it with rags. In about half an hour, the rice's residual heat made it soft and sticky and ready to serve. But there was little heat left in the blood seeping through Father's feet. His heels remained dry and cracked no matter how long they were kept in the rags.

Earlier that morning Mother had been hired by a family to wash their sheets and clothes. She had said she wouldn't come back until evening and asked me to take care of Father.

I panfried a bowlful of rice for Father. Father's teeth were almost all gone, so the wrinkles of his cheeks seemed to work harder than his jaws. They rolled and wiggled like an octopus, and then the dish was empty. I took it away, but Father still held his hands in the air, waiting for the bowl to return. I snatched up a towel and wiped a circle around his mouth. Father got the message and lowered his hands disappointedly.

I cleared off the table and laid out two bags of white pigment powder. An inexpensive interior paint could be prepared by mixing the powder with water. I was planning to paint the walls and ceiling of the attic. White could create a visual illusion of spaciousness, I believed.

While I was dusting off the wall beside the north window, I heard a strange noise coming out of Father's mouth.

I turned back and saw Father's head sinking into his chest. I dropped the broom and rushed toward him. I was going to straighten his head, but my arms would not reach out.

When Father took a nap, his head always turned around clockwise—nodding toward his right side a few times, then toward his back for a few strokes, then left, and then forward. The forward nods took the shortest time. With a few rumblings in his throat, his head would quickly switch to the right for the next cycle. If his head bent forward for too long, Father would be at risk of suffocation.

Father had nearly suffocated once for that reason. Nobody was at home. Luckily, his body was off balance and he fell over. That saved his life.

We brought Father to the hospital to get a checkup. The doctor fumbled with his fingers in the lizard-like skin on Father's neck, and the diagnosis was made: he was old. The doctor told me that the cricoid cartilage, a ring-shaped piece of gristle that protected the wind pipe in Father's throat, was "weathered." When his neck bent forward, the wind pipe was flattened and his breath was cut off. Usually, the patient adjusted his neck by himself. Occasionally, he needed a little help from others— simply to lift up his chin.

My hand almost touched Father's hairy chin. A simple nudge would bring the breath back into Father's lungs, but my hands were frozen in the air.

Father's face turned dark red. The scar on his left cheek was swollen and shiny. The scar had been there for almost ten years. When Father was sixty-nine years old, he fell down while pushing a cart over a bridge.

With a slight jog on the chin, Father would have been saved. But to my surprise, my hand withdrew from Father's jaw. As if repulsed by an opposing magnetic field, my feet were pushed back, while my eyes still gazed at the blue veins bulging at Father's temples.

I jerked the trapdoor open and dashed down the stairs.

I ran down the sidewalk.

The sun shone like an electric arc, overexposing the world. The bells of bicycles sounded like alarms. Gradually, the streaming bicycles became muted, sliding away like a school of fish.

I stumbled into a movie theater. I sat in the dark, listening to the pounding of my heart.

I bent forward. My head pressed against the seat in front of me. My hands gripped the back of my head. My body began to ache. My legs grew sore, and then my back. Father whacked me with a rod. My arms went numb. Yes, Father was fierce when he beat his sons. Unlike Mother, he never slapped his kids with his hands. He used a rod, a chestnut rod around two feet long, one inch thick. The twisted grain of the branch was black and glossy.

As if he were beating dogs—no, wolves—Father beat Bao, beat Ling, and beat me. On the way to its targets, the flying weapon occasionally destroyed peripheral objects like light-bulbs, glasses, and thermos bottles, but Father's punishment was never interrupted or diverted.

After the beatings, as was his routine, Father ordered us to approach him. With his pliers-like fingers, Father squeezed each swollen bump to see if any bones were broken.

Chuen, you were lucky. You never got that treatment from Father. Maybe by the time you were sturdy enough to withstand the rod, Father was too old to swing the weapon. Chuen, I envy you.

I closed my eyes. In the dark I saw a little girl.

Carrying a pillow, trembling all over, the little girl entered a bedroom.

The little girl was my mother. She was seven years old. Her parents, studying chemistry in Japan for a couple of years, left their daughter to live with her aunt and uncle, Mother told me.

Her grandmother was dying. She suffered from a strange disease. Her chest ached terribly, but she just wouldn't die. She wheezed noisily, day and night.

The whole family came. It was a large family; more than a hundred relatives crowded into the big house. In the beginning, people were crying. But three or four days passed, and her grandmother still wheezed, showing no signs of expiring.

It was the busy season for peasants, and the relatives became impatient. Some said that grandmother must have something left unsettled on her mind. But others said that there must be ghosts blocking the way and the demons wouldn't let you go unless you paid them a fee. People thought the latter idea sounded more plausible. So a few monks were summoned to chant the sutras, and wads of hell money (symbolic bills offered to the spirits for use in the afterlife) were burned. But it did not work. The grandmother still wheezed and still did not want to go. The relatives got angry.

"It seems to me . . ." Granduncle, the eldest of the family, thought aloud. His shrunken lips wiggled and writhed until finally a decision was made: "She needs help from a child."

My mother was chosen.

There were other children in the family, but they were too young to offer help. There was another reason my mother was chosen—she was female. Females, with long hair and short minds, would always be granted the forgiveness of the Buddha, no matter what stupid things they had done.

Granduncle asked my mother to approach. He tied a red ribbon in her hair, saying that the red knot would ward off evils. Granduncle gave her half a silver ingot, a reward for her service. Then he told her how to help.

That scared the little girl. She cried loudly and threw the silver ingot to the ground. She ran back to her uncle, but he offered no refuge. Instead, he gave her a few "chestnuts"—raps on her head with his knuckles—and she still had to go help her grandmother.

Holding a pillow in her arms and escorted by her uncle, she walked toward the bedroom, quivering all over.

The room was dark and it stank. Mother told me that it

smelled like a decaying corpse. Something in her grandmother's body was rotting away. The girl approached the bed, holding the pillow in front of her. She called in a shaking voice, "Grandma . . ."

No response.

Her grandmother's eyeballs were covered by sagging eyelids. Nothing moved except the sunken cheeks, which slowly ebbed and flowed. Her uncle gave the girl a poke in the back. She lifted the pillow, bringing it to her grandmother's face. She was about to press down the pillow when she heard a shriek! The dried lips opened wide. A black hole. Two eyeballs bulged out, staring at the girl.

The little girl fled.

"Good-for-nothing!" Her uncle picked up the pillow that had been dropped on the floor and pushed it against the dying woman's face.

"Weird. It was really weird." Every time Mother talked about things in her hometown, she slid into a strong Hunan dialect. "Her eyes were closed. I saw it. How did she know I was going to press down the pillow?"

The Chinese traditionally send good wishes to loved ones, such as "Live as long as ten thousand years." To me, however, that is a vicious curse. Even if you enjoy happiness for a hundred years, for the rest of the nine thousand nine hundred years you have to lie in your bed alone. You can listen to the insects call from the window, but you have to smell the urine that soaks the bed. Flies can lay their droppings on your eyelids, but you can't even touch your own toes. Though you have somebody to feed you three times a day, the food that gets into your bowels is not digested. Instead, it rots and becomes the pus oozing out of your bedsores day by day, month by month, year by year.

Yes, you do have visitors. Generation after generation, your offspring hold their breath when they come to see you. And generation after generation, your great-great-grandchildren dash out the door and cheer for their short lives!

I looked down at the glowing seat light.

A huge eyeball gazed at me.

In the dirt yard in front of my father's barn, a water buffalo was going to be slaughtered. It was Hunchback's buffalo. It had gotten old, too old to plow. Retired buffalo could still do some easy jobs, like turning a grindstone. But that was a donkey's job. A buffalo ate much more hay than a donkey did. So the best way to deal with a retired buffalo was to kill it. All the neighborhood kids, with shaved heads, exposed bottoms, and bare feet, stood around the yard.

I was one of them.

Four poles were stuck into the ground. The yard was swept and sprinkled with water. Hunchback led his buffalo into the yard. He fed it a handful of hay and watched as the buffalo ate its last dinner. While the buffalo was chewing its food, four ropes were tied to its legs. Each rope was held by a man. Hunchback led the buffalo to the center of the poles. The buffalo was still chewing idly.

Somebody shouted an order. The four men pulled the ropes

simultaneously and looped them around the poles. The legs of the buffalo splayed apart. The beast was terrified and trembling. Its eyes opened wide, looking to its master for help. Hunchback put his hands on the buffalo's head and sobbed.

Gold Teeth, the blacksmith of the village, swaggered into the scene. He carried a huge hammer on his shoulder as he strode toward the buffalo. He swept the sobbing Hunchback aside. He spit on his hands and rubbed the saliva over his palms. He spread his legs with the left foot a half-step forward. He raised the hammer high above his head; the shiny metal caught the sun. He shouted. Accelerated by the muscles of his waist and arms, the hammer crashed down.

Thud!

The skull of the buffalo indented. The forelegs slowly bent. The poles quaked and tilted. The buffalo knelt by increments, and then his head hit the ground.

And it peed.

The kids edged closer and closer.

No blood. Not a single drop of blood. On the head, the spot hit by the hammer popped up.

A huge eyeball gazed at me.

Mushrooms, a cluster of wild mushrooms, bright and colorful, shimmered in the dark.

Go away, you poisonous fungi. I did not get your help then, and now I don't need your help anymore.

Father, I remember that once when you brought Bao and me to the suburbs to collect wild vegetables, I saw some colorful mushrooms growing in the grass. Bao warned me not to touch them, saying that they were poisonous. But even though I did not touch them, my mind was poisoned anyway. Many years later, I read an article by chance in *Popular Medicine*—"Identification of Poisonous Mushrooms." I cut out the color illustration and put it in a lockbox. I lost track of how many times I gazed at those vivid photographs.

"Ghost's cap" is blood red, "drunk bear" is bright yellow and "cat's pupil" is shiny green. The article said that the toxins in these mushrooms are nerve poisons. The symptoms are dizziness, double vision, and hallucinations, and usually result in suffocation due to a paralysis of the nerves in the breathing muscles. The extreme complexity of the poisons' chemistry makes them very difficult to identify in a patient's urine or blood by conventional tests.

Father, all the energy in your life is exhausted. The time left holds nothing but suffering. Why don't you find a way to escape? A small piece of "cat's pupil" would be quite enough to make you doze off. No pain, no struggle. Probably you would hallucinate, but aren't hallucinations a kind of dream? Father, you often dreamed, dreamed about your childhood, dreamed about your hometown. Dreams became your only source of pleasure and comfort. Father, why don't you give yourself a super dream? Let all the sweet memories explode like fireworks and then quietly fade away!

Father, I know you are too old to go to the suburbs to collect wild vegetables again. But I can go. I can pick the mushrooms for you. When spring comes, I'll go and pick a few of them, and put a single one in your noodle soup. Eat the soup, warm and delicious, and go back to your bed. You'll be set forever. If there is a heaven, you are qualified to go there. If there is no heaven in the sky, at least you will be spared the hell on earth.

Father, you are almost eighty years old; you would die quietly. No crying, no struggle, and nobody would suspect anything wrong. Father, your son is an atheist to the bone, not believing in God or demons, paying no attention to retribution or judgment. I am safe, as safe as the void; I am protected, protected by nothing. If worse comes to worst, if a God or demons do exist, if there is such a thing as retribution or judgment, what can they do to me? I do nothing wrong. What your son would do is exactly the grand release the Buddha will eventually grant to all good people.

Again and again I rehearsed my plan. And again and again I regretted that I did not act upon it. I waited and waited. In the winter I waited for the spring. In the spring I waited for a summer thundershower. In the summer I thought maybe the mushrooms in the fall would be even richer and riper . . .

Finally, Father, I don't need to feel any more shame for my delay, for my hesitation, and for my cowardliness. The chance drops from heaven!

Suddenly the lights in the movie theater came up. I staggered out of the building. I felt unsteady, as if I was standing on the deck of a rolling boat.

I passed the former Full & Happy restaurant. It had become a general store many years ago, selling wares like soaps, tissues, matches, and candles. The setting sun reflected in the shopwindows set the store on fire. I turned my head away from the glare and I saw my father.

Father was running. Clutching a big bowl, he was running

awkwardly toward the end of a long line. The line started from the Full & Happy Restaurant, meandered down the sidewalk of Penglai Road, turned the corner, and disappeared into Temple of Letters Road.

Steam rose from the big barrel of bean dregs paste.

Father dissolved like a mirage, but I heard Father's panting, Father's coughing, and Father's heart beating.

I stood in the middle of Penglai Road.

A truck suddenly materialized in front of me, but I did not hear the honking and the squeal of its brakes. The furious driver jumped off the truck and shouted at me. I stared at his twisted lips, as if I was watching a fish in a tank. He hit me on the shoulder. With a jerk, I turned and started to run, run toward home.

My lungs sucked with a hissing noise, but no air could flow in. My face was burning, but my heart was frozen into a crystal of ice. I ran and ran, but I did not feel my feet touching the ground. I was dashing through the sky. Buildings blurred into two bands of cirrus clouds and whistling air pulled my earlobes into a pair of contrails.

I crashed through the front door. I bounced upstairs and exploded open the attic door.

Father sat there.

He was not taking his nap. He was sitting beside the stove. Clutching a spatula, Father was frying the white paint powder in the pan.

Two torn bags were left on the table.

There was a graze on his forehead and dried blood on his left cheek. He must have fallen over.

Father did not notice me. He concentrated on his own business. He stuck his fingers in the pan, testing the temperature of the powder. With shaking fingers, he tweezed up a little and brought it toward his mouth. I swept the powder off his hand. Father turned.

A pair of opaque pupils stared at me.

I held my father by his shoulders.

And I cried.

CHAPTER THIRTY-ONE

Rubber Plantation

In the summer of 1966 my sister, Chuen, graduated from middle school. The government's campaign advocating that students settle down in the countryside was in full swing. Chuen was sixteen. Eight years before, when my brother Ling left for Gansu Province, he had been sixteen, too. But Chuen was going even farther away—the Dai Minority Autonomous Region in Yunnan Province, bordering Laos and Vietnam.

Mother felt sad, but my sister was excited. Chuen had been enraptured by the tropical scenes she saw in movies: bamboo houses, reed rafts, banana trees, sugarcane, mangoes, monkeys, hornbills . . .

The rubber plantation to which Chuen was assigned was run by the local army. So Chuen made a green uniform with a canvas belt, which gave her girlish figure a military air. Our family's political situation had not allowed her to join the Red Guard while she was in school. But now, willy-nilly, she was to become a member of a rubber plantation belonging to the Peoples' Liberation Army!

In her homemade uniform, Chuen rushed upstairs and down all day like a character in a slapstick silent movie. Mother prepared bag after bag of food for her daughter, but Chuen yelled at her:

"You're crazy, Mom! Yunnan is a tropical rain forest. Any time you want a banana, you just reach out your hand. And it's hard to avoid tripping over the pineapple plants. Catfish crawl out of the pond every night. Why are you making me take this stinky, salted fish? And the dried meat, yuk! It looks just like sliced boot!"

I knew that Yunnan was a richly endowed province. In our neighborhood, quite a few students had been given assignments in Inner Mongolia, Xinjiang, and Gansu. Compared with those northern territories, it wouldn't be exaggerating to say that Chuen's plantation was heaven's backyard.

The only thing I worried about was the snakes. I bought a book entitled *Prevention and Treatment of Poisonous Snakebites* for my sister. The book listed roughly a dozen varieties of poisonous snakes found in China—Yunnan Province had almost all of them: pit vipers, cobras, asps, rattlesnakes . . . The most dreaded among them was the giant cobra, which inhabited the rain forests of southern Yunnan. The adult snake could reach ten feet in length and was known to actively attack human beings. When provoked, the snake could spit venom a distance of six feet. Bitten by the giant cobra, you have only two choices: death or disability.

Following the information in the appendix of the book, I collected all kinds of medications for snakebite: Chinese herbs, Western medicines, pills, ampoules, internal remedies, and external pastes. I packed them in a large bag. I was confident that there was enough, even if Chuen's entire battalion was attacked by cobras.

I ran simulations with my sister of the "crosscut-and-suction" technique for treating snakebites. A fountain pen stood in for the scalpel. I drew scores of red crosses on her hands and feet, which were the areas most susceptible to snake attack. She practiced first aid techniques like squeezing, sucking, and flushing very seriously. Once she was practicing tourniquets so earnestly that she unhesitatingly tore up a brand-new white shirt. But two years later my sister was crippled nonetheless.

The rubber plantation was run by the army, so my sister's address was a code: Fourth Company, Fourth Battalion, First Regiment, Third Division, 8376 Army.

For the first two months, Chuen's letters read like poetry loaded with zillions of adjectives. Language was not enough; photos were rushed to assist. In the pictures she stuck her head out a window of the bamboo house as if she was listening to an exotic bird calling. And she posed with her neck stretched upward under the banana trees, suggesting tons of fruit hanging just out of the frame. And she plunged a mango right up to the lens, convincing us that the fruit weighed at least a thousand pounds.

Among the pictures, the one showing her tapping rubber trees was the most impressive. Wearing a battery lamp helmet, she held a knife with both hands and gouged the trunk of the tree. Chuen wrote that tapping rubber trees must be done before sunrise. The sap flows only before the dewdrops dry. I believe the picture was taken by flashlight: the v-shaped gouge flared, showing its razor-sharp blade.

But starting in the third month, maybe because of the end of the rainy season there, the contents of Chuen's letters dried up drastically.

It is hard to believe, but in those years even the rain forests of Yunnan were plagued by famine. The blue mountains, clear brooks, and singing birds in Chuen's letters were completely replaced by salted fish, dehydrated pickles, and preserved meats. She needed them, needed them badly.

But in Shanghai's post offices, big posters clearly forbade, from fear of contamination, the mailing of any food, even if it was salted or preserved. Mother knew her daughter wouldn't open her mouth unless she was desperate. So sending a parcel of food became an action similar to a terrorist's espionage operation.

Mother would bring the parcel to the window of the post office for inspection. In the wrapping cloth were a few books, clothes, and a pair of foam sandals. No problem. The mailing form was stamped "checked."

Then Mother took the checked package to the table in a corner of the post office to sew it up. I was there waiting. When Mother reached the table, I took an identical parcel from my bag—same cloth, same size, and same weight. But inside, the contents were exactly what was forbidden by the poster above our heads. With a little maneuvering, we switched parcels. Mother sewed up my package, wrote out the address on the wrapping cloth, and handed it in at the window.

The clerk checked the size and weight; they were the same as the figures on the form. She squeezed the bulges on the sewed-up parcel. Under the wrapping cloth lurked salted meat cut to the same shape and size as the foam sandals. All right, the contents matched the description on the form. With a toss, the parcel landed in the canvas mail bag. In two months or so Chuen would get it.

Mother was extremely cautious. She would put the salted meat and fish into layer after layer of plastic bags. Each bag was individually sealed to avoid leaking grease and odors. Then the plastic-wrapped contents were put in a leatherette pouch to prevent breakage. Mother would repackage pickled vegetables from their original glass bottles into plastic containers, each sealed with wax. She would boil soy sauce until it condensed into a block of asphalt. In two years Mother's clandestine operation was never discovered.

Mother tried very hard to help her daughter overcome the food shortage, but she never imagined that the worst problem was not nutrition.

In her letters, Chuen did not complain about anything except the lack of food, but I had a hunch that something else was wrong.

A girl from the same company as Chuen was stricken with acute hepatitis and sent back to Shanghai for treatment. In a letter my sister asked me to visit the invalid. From Chuen's sick friend I learned something that was inconvenient for her to write home about.

The plantation leaders at all levels were demobilized soldiers or officers from the local army of the Yunnan military bloc.

Since the plantation was run by the army, the lifestyle was a military one. The arrangement of jobs, the distribution of housing, the setting of wages, and so on and so forth—everything was determined by the officers. But for the young workers, far from home for the first time in their lives, who had not seen their parents for more than a year, the most urgent item was getting leave to visit their families. The commander, of course, held the power to grant or deny permission for leaves. And the chance of getting permission was strongly influenced by a girl's attitude on the night she went to the commander's office to hand in her application.

Now and then, there were cases of resistance. Complaints were submitted to higher levels. The superior, however, was quite probably the one who gave the harassing officer his job in the first place; maybe he had even introduced him to the Party. So after a little commotion, the complaints were always dismissed for lack of sufficient evidence.

Three girls in the Seventh Company were determined to flee. They climbed over mountains and gorges and escaped from the plantation. Eventually, they reached the Jingpu River along the border of the autonomous region. There were soldiers posted day and night on the steel bridge that spanned the river. No one passed without a travel permit. Hungry and tired, the girls waited in the small town beside the bridge, not knowing what to do.

The autonomous region produced no fuel of its own; all fuel was imported by tank trucks from Kunming, the capital of Yunnan Province. That day an empty tank truck was returning to Kunming. The driver had stopped to rest in the town where the girls waited. Seeing the driver enter a restaurant, the three girls stealthily climbed onto the truck, crawled through the hatch, and descended into the tank.

After his meal the driver drove his truck onto the bridge, where he was stopped by a soldier. The driver thought it was a routine inspection, but the soldier pointed to the flapping cover and said that it wasn't safe to leave the hatch open. So the driver slammed the cover shut and twisted the lock closed. Then he continued his northward journey.

Two days later he arrived in Kunming. He took his usual three days off and went to fill the tank in preparation for his next run. He climbed up the tank and opened the hatch. A miasma burst forth. They had to cut the tank open to remove the bloated bodies.

News of the incident was circulated throughout the plantation as a warning of the consequences of desertion.

The girl told me about another case, too.

A few hills to the south of the Fourth Company, in which my sister served, lay the territory of the Third Battalion. A girl in the Third Battalion got pregnant. Assuming that her protruding belly provided solid evidence, the girl pressed suit against the commander of the battalion. The girl focused on her revenge single-mindedly, not realizing that her immediate superior, the company commander, had placed her under round-the-clock surveillance.

As an old Chinese detective story puts it, "You must catch a pair to prove an affair," and the company commander executed the classic strategy perfectly. One night the girl and her boyfriend were caught and dragged from the bushes. They had enlisted together back in their hometown, Kunming. He now worked on the road team as a dynamiter.

Before being sent to a labor reform camp, the unlucky couple was paraded around the battalion and subjected to lengthy *dou,* a unique combination of shouting, accusations, and jostling. Their crime was twofold: illegal sexuality and slander against their revolutionary leader. Because the labor camp to which she was sentenced was not equipped to take care of pregnant women and infants, it was necessary to clean up the girl before she was dispatched.

On the day of the abortion, the entire battalion was assembled on the drill field in front of the hospital. Each associated unit had sent representatives to observe the proceedings. Officers from all levels of the battalion, including the accused battalion commander and the meritorious company commander, sat on two long benches placed on either side of the window of the operating room. They faced the battalion, symbolizing the solidarity and strength of their collective leadership.

Speeches were made. Then came the operation. Abruptly, the bamboo shutters of the operating room were thrown open. In full view of the entire battalion, the abortion began. The shrieking girl had been tied to the operating table. Hundreds of teenagers, standing in formation on the drill field, held their breaths and listened.

Everything was going smoothly until the unexpected occurred—the boyfriend escaped from the brig.

You couldn't expect a jury-rigged jail in the country to be as sturdy as the First Shanghai Prison. The brig was nothing but a bamboo cage plastered with mud. It was "enough to stop a gentleman, but not a thief," as locally made locks were described. Serving time in that kind of cell relied heavily on your "revolutionary conscience."

Clearly, the boyfriend knew he would never be a gentleman. With a single kick, he smashed a hole through the wall. He crawled out of the cage and ran to the battalion warehouse. Nobody was inside. He opened a trunk and grabbed a dozen sticks the size of relay batons. He tied them to his belt.

The boy made his way to the back door of the hospital and hid himself in the bushes. When the girl's soprano hit its highest notes, he made his entrance. He leaped out of the bushes, rushed toward the operating room, and desperately attempted to jump through the window. Nobody knew his intentions. A plausible guess was that he wanted to spring his girlfriend from the operation and escape with her. Or maybe he had simply gone crazy. Anyway, he was caught by the officers as they leaped off the benches. He struggled but couldn't move. The meritorious company commander felt something around the boy's waist. He lifted the trespasser's shirt and immediately shouted:

"Hit the dirt!"

But he was the only one to hit the dirt.

All the other leaders were baffled—there were no bombers diving, no tanks rumbling. Hit the dirt? For what? Well, you can debate and discuss to your heart's content, but dynamite won't wait. Bang! The operating room splintered into a hail of bamboo shoots.

The good news was that the teenagers standing on the field were not actively involved. While the officers wrestled with the fugitive, they stayed clear of the leaders' seats. The formation remained precise. They were stunned by the explosion, but no one was injured.

The lovers were finished on the spot, saving themselves any further trouble. The leaders, excepting the officer who hit the ground, all died heroes' deaths. For soldiers, shedding blood is their bounden duty. Only the doctor was blown apart for no reason. He was a good doctor. When one of his severed arms was dug out from the debris, the blackened fingers still clutched the stainless steel curette.

Maybe the losses to our side were too heavy and could potentially boost the enemy's spirits; the plantation did not publicize the case. Only one notice was circulated among all the companies. It required greater restrictions on access to explosive materials. But hundreds witnessed the event that day. The hero's exploits shook the whole plantation.

The Kunmingese, girls and boys both, had the reputation of being sissies (perhaps owing to the region's balmy weather). But that big bang expanded their stature like popcorn. In the pecking order they jumped above even the Beijingese, who were always snobs about their royal roots in the capital city.

Right after the explosion, one girl picked up a shred of bamboo that had landed at her feet. She carved it into a heart and wore it around her neck for the rest of her years of service in the battalion.

The company commander escaped death, but he was paralyzed. With contorted mouth and eyes, he murmured his words, spittle leaking from his lips.

One line of a sutra states, "When a man is dying, his words become kind." The commander was half-dead, so he was more or less enlightened. Tied to his wheelchair, he was wheeled through the army hospital hallways. Nurses became accustomed to his language:

"Sh-sh-shit! Th-that whole th-thing had nothing to do with me. Why the f-fuck was I s-so gung ho? Sh-sh-shi . . ."

Chuen wanted to come home, but she didn't dare tell Mother. Instead, she wrote to me. I wrote back, asking her to indicate, on a scale of one to ten, her determination to return. Chuen responded immediately. I opened the envelope. Three large numerals, written in blood:

100

CHAPTER THIRTY-TWO

My Injury

I was determined to help my sister return home, but I didn't know what I could do for her. Coming from a family like ours, it was simply impossible to curry favors from government officials. And I did not dare pass Bao's motto about fighting on to my sister. If I told her, "What the hell, just go!" she might jump into the Jingpu River the night she got my advice.

The old saying goes, "Every inch of the country is under the emperor's feet." Even if she was lucky enough to evade the soldiers stationed on the bridge and make it back to Shanghai, she still wouldn't be able to escape the siege that would be laid by the local consolidation team.

The consolidation teams were created to deal with ex-students who returned to the cities from settlements in the countryside without authorization. A consolidation team was organized by each block's residents' committee. Retired workers were the core of the teams.

Understanding that the settlement of young people in the

208

countryside was a strategy vital to the future of the revolution, the elderly team members showed great enthusiasm for their work. Three shifts in turn, twenty-four hours a day, seven days a week, they sat in your home, patiently practicing persuasion. They would relate revolutionary history from the Paris Commune right down to the People's Commune. They would bring a *huchin,* a Chinese violin with two ox tendon strings, and sing a selection of revolutionary Peking opera songs for you and your family. Those who couldn't sing would beat gongs and drums, shaking the dust from your ceiling and window panes.

The residents' committee had a tight budget. Each persuader only received twenty cents "tea allowance" per day to compensate for the heavy loss of saliva. But facing a roomful of scalps gleaming with sweat and oil, you knew you didn't stand a chance.

Yet there were some exceptional conditions that could rescue you: hepatitis with a GPT in excess of one thousand, or nephritis if the white blood cells completely covered the microscope field. To screen out goldbrickers, members of the residents' committee would suddenly descend and escort you to the hospital in order to personally supervise the medical tests. They would watch the syringe suck the blood from your veins, or put their ears to the bathroom door to listen as you peed into the sample cup. Permission to stay would not be granted unless the tests were repeated satisfactorily three times.

In my freshman year of college, I took a course in U.S. history. I was surprised by the spirit of the European immigrants who explored and opened the western territories. The barbarity of the new continent in the seventeenth century was far beyond that of Inner Mongolia, Xinjiang, or Yunnan in the twentieth century. But those immigrants didn't seem to need anyone to recite revolutionary history or sing revolutionary opera to them. When the previous family had been attacked and a scalped body lay draped over a charred wheel by the roadside, the families that followed still drove their wagons, slowly and steadily, toward the setting sun.

That history course did not convince me that the exploration of the American West was the apex of human civilization, but at least it was the law of the jungle in action—the weak preyed upon by the strong. Killing or being killed, eating or being eaten, each side of the struggle hoped it would be the stronger.

What I had seen, however, bluntly defied Darwinism. I frequently witnessed pale-faced ex-students sitting on a bench outside the hospital lab, waiting for test results. They were embroiled in the lengthy process of acquiring authorization to stay. The candidates stared at the small window in the lab door, hoping that particular organs in their bodies would not suddenly stop rotting.

Being raised and having lived more than twenty years in the attic, I did not expect much privacy. But after I received my sister's last letter, I suddenly became concerned about having my own space.

Under the north window of the attic, where Father and I slept, I built a compartment out of particleboard to separate Father and myself. The tallest part of my triangular cell was just high enough to allow me to sit up. A thick beam ran across the ceiling of my chamber. I hung a lamp from the beam. The deep lampshade permitted only a vertical shaft of light to escape. It spotlighted a short-legged table like the Japanese use. Its height allowed me to sit with my legs folded underneath it. While I slept, the table rode across my waist. I crawled in and out of my cell through a small door. And I put a steel lock on it.

I didn't ask my parents for permission to build the compartment. I did not even bother to offer them an explanation. Father did not raise any objections. He could no longer see, and most of his hearing was gone. Since he slept with his body curled, the reduced space did not bother him too much. Worried, Mother watched me for a few weeks, but saw nothing abnormal enough to warrant her interference.

Every day after work, I crawled into my cell and read. In the corner of my chamber I piled my old textbooks. Some medical books, like *The Physician's Handbook* and *The Complete Guide to Surgery,* were mixed into the piles. My childhood wish had been to study medicine, and collecting a few medical texts was a quite natural offshoot of my interest.

I bought a box of acid resistant bottles from the laboratory glass supply store. There were twenty bottles in the box, each held 25 milliliters and came with a tapered glass stopper. I also acquired a few measuring cups, funnels, syringes, and a precise scale.

Then I bought a cage of six white mice from the pet store. Like pet lovers everywhere, I installed an exercise wheel in the cage. But my tiny pets were ill-fated; soon their legs could no longer spin the wheel.

Stealthily, I collected a variety of strong corrosives from my factory: sulfuric acid, hydrofluoric acid, hydrochloric acid, nitric acid, prussic acid, glacial acetic acid, and lye. I took the samples back to my secret lab. I diluted the corrosives into solutions of varying potencies, decanted them into the acid resistant bottles, and labeled each of them.

I went to the butcher and bought a half-pound of lean pork leg meat. I diced it into chunks weighing about one gram apiece. These I dropped into the bottles containing the different concentrations, and I observed the corrosive effect of each solution.

I thought one of the acids might be the best choice, but my comprehensive screening unexpectedly proved that the 15% solution of lye had the strongest effect on the meat. At a temperature of 37° C, the meat had lost its elasticity one hour after immersion; the muscle fiber had expanded and loosened. It looked like it had been thoroughly boiled.

The right corrosive and appropriate concentration had been chosen; now the proper dosage had to be determined. I tested the 15% lye solution on the mice. With a 1 ml syringe, I injected 0.1 ml into the left hind leg of the first mouse, 0.2 ml into the same limb of the second mouse, and 0.3 ml into the third. During the injection I held the mouse's mouth to prevent it from squeaking—Mother was sleeping on the other side of the attic.

That was on Saturday evening. All night I sat and observed the results of the test. Five minutes after the injections, the mice started to tremble. Half an hour later the mouse who had received 0.3 ml died. Three hours later the one who had been injected with 0.2 ml lay motionless. Only the mouse who had received 0.1 ml continued to tremble. The next morning it dragged its blackened left leg and drank water like crazy. The mouse continued to live for three more days before it finally succumbed.

I cut off its left leg and found that the dead muscle had already begun to rot. The direct cause of death was obviously not the corrosion from the lye, but the rotting of the dead muscle and the resultant blood poisoning from the decay. But before the blood poisoning took the mouse's life, three days had passed. I believed it was enough leeway.

Then I injected the same amount of solution into the fourth mouse's leg. Two hours later, I dissected it alive. I found that the muscle had darkened, and closely matched the color of gangrenous tissue shown in the *Compendium of Illustrated Surgical Operations*. I repeated the test with the remaining two mice. The results were nearly identical. I concluded that the goal of my experiments on animals had been achieved.

The designated target, however, was not a mouse but a human. So I had to test the solution in a human body.

On February 4, 1972, around four o'clock in the afternoon, I reported to the clinic in my factory with a minor injury. A nail had punctured the middle toe of my right foot. The doctor said the wound was not serious, painted it with Mercurochrome, and told me to inform him of any subsequent symptoms.

That night when I got home, I prepared a basin of warm water and washed my feet. Then I crawled into my "biological lab." I lay flat on my back. I recalled the entire sequence of my experiments. I felt confident.

The clock struck ten.

I listened to make sure Father and Mother had fallen asleep. Silently, I bolted the door. I pulled down the lamp. Then, from a small wooden box, I withdrew a syringe and a bottle of prepared 15% lye solution. I sucked 0.1 ml of the solution into the syringe. I had already measured the volume of flesh on the pad of my middle toe. Its volume was the same as that of the white mouse's hind leg, so the dosage would be the same.

I felt my heart palpitate.

I closed my eyes and meditated, waiting for my breathing to calm. Then I lifted my right foot and injected the 0.1 ml solution into the tip of my middle toe.

I lay down. I looked at the alarm clock—quarter past ten. I covered myself with the blanket. I concentrated on my sensations. It didn't hurt. There was only a little itching at the point of injection. I kept myself from scratching it. Gradually, the itching faded away. It faded too much; all feeling had disappeared. I tried to wiggle the toe. I could hear the rustling of the skin against the mat, but there was no feeling in the digit.

Precisely like the mice, five minutes after the injection I started to tremble. The trembling rose from my right foot, crept up the thigh, and spread through my whole body. My teeth chattered, but I wasn't surprised or scared. I knew that, like the mice, I would be trembling all night. I felt cold. I wrapped myself tighter in the blanket and, counting my breaths, calmly fell asleep.

I don't remember if I dreamed about anything.

The next morning I limped to the factory clinic. I lifted my right foot for the doctor's inspection. The front segment of my middle toe was black. The doctor was shocked. He ran downstairs, grabbed a driver, and sent me to the Seventh Hospital.

In the emergency room, the surgeon immediately diagnosed me: "Acute infection from injury. Local tissue necrosis." And immediately he cut off the blackened section on the underside of my middle toe. Then he injected me with large doses of antibiotics and anti-blood-poisoning serum to prevent the infection from invading my whole body.

I stayed in the observation room of the hospital overnight. I left a message on the neighborhood telephone, telling my parents that I was spending the night at the factory on guard duty. No whole-body symptoms developed. The surgeon admired my immune system and released me.

The factory clinic changed my dressing every day. After about a month the wound had healed. The toe shrank from the loss of muscle and other tissue, curving downward like a chicken claw.

I had succeeded.

A few days after my wound healed, I sent a letter to my sister. In the letter I enclosed a sample of my calligraphy written in small characters. I wrote that I hoped she would find the time to practice calligraphy from my example. Chuen wrote back indignantly, saying I must be joking. Ignoring her anger, I sent her a second sample of my calligraphy.

I knew my sister was smart. She finally decoded the contents—I had written my plan in two parts. The first piece of calligraphy contained the odd-numbered characters, the even-numbered characters constituted the second sample. Chuen responded. The letter contained only one word:

"Agreed."

On April 13, I sent a package to Chuen. No salted fish or dried meat. I did not need any tricks to fool the post office, either. In the package was a box of penicillin and a syringe. In those days sending medicine to the countryside was officially encouraged and was a popular practice. But the aluminum lid of one of the six bottles of penicillin had a barely noticeable hole in it. The color of that bottle's contents was slightly different— it was not penicillin, but 2 ml of 15% lye solution.

The target of the next injection would have a volume twenty times that of the tip of my middle toe.

CHAPTER THIRTY-THREE

I Am Hunted

After the parcel was mailed, I spent the two most dreadful months of my life. I was haunted by unceasing nightmares. Strange to say, some of the nightmares were even wet dreams. I dreamed that a snake wound itself around me and I swelled within the deadly coils. Finally, the fangs punctured my body, yet what ejected the venom was myself. I frequently awakened with a start at midnight. With wide-open eyes, I would lie flat in the dark, feeling the pounding of my heart against my rib cage.

On June 26, just before dawn, the sound of a motorcycle's exhaust stopped abruptly in front of our building. I heard somebody yelling from the street:

"Telegram for Cao Guanlong!"

I jumped up, hitting my head on the beam. I rushed downstairs.

The delivery man said, "Give me your name-seal."

I snatched the telegram out of his grip. My fingers trembled so violently that I could hardly tear open the envelope.

"Give me your name-seal. Do you hear me?" the man repeated.

I stared at him, my hands shaking.

"Idiot." The man grabbed my thumb, plunged it into the red seal ink, and pressed a smudgy fingerprint on his form. Then, trailing black smoke, the motorcycle zoomed away.

I held my breath and tore open the envelope. Under the streetlight, a line of the telegram jumped out:

CHUEN SICK, CRITICAL CONDITION.

The rubber plantation had sent the telegram.

The red ink from my thumb stained the slip. Clad in only my underpants, I stood, numbed. I turned my head to find Mother standing beside me. Mother took the telegram, turned toward the light, and read aloud one word after another. Then she collapsed on the sidewalk.

Frantic, Mother wanted to leave for Yunnan at once. But I knew that even if you flew to Kunming, the capital of Yunnan, there was still a four-day-and-four-night bus ride to get to the rubber plantation. I grabbed Mother and said, "Let's wait, wait . . ."

Wait for what? I didn't know myself.

At last, on the evening of the third day, we received a second telegram from the rubber plantation:

CONDITION OF CHUEN NO LONGER CRITICAL.

On the fifth day we got Chuen's telegram:

I AM OKAY. WILL RETURN SHANGHAI SOON.

Twenty days later my whole family went to meet Chuen at the railway station. Chuen's left hand was heavily wrapped in gauze, her arm supported by a sling. Her face was pale, but she looked elated. She laughed, reached out her good hand, and waved it in front of Mother's face, as if testing a patient's eye response.

In the past month, Mother had shriveled.

Chuen told us that one day, at dawn, she had gone to tap the rubber trees. She tripped on something, and the gouge pricked her left palm. It was a common injury; she paid no attention to it and continued her work. Unexpectedly, she became feverish that night and almost lost consciousness.

The girl in the lower bunk was awakened by Chuen's shaking. She ran out and brought back the battalion doctor. The doctor lifted her left hand and was shocked—her palm was totally black. Hastily, they rushed Chuen to the 2040th Army Field Hospital. The hospital, on the Burmese border, treated Chinese soldiers sent back from the Indochina battle zones.

Debridement was immediately performed on the injured area. The surgeon cut all the dead tissue from Chuen's hand. Large doses of antibiotics and anti-blood-poisoning serum were administered to prevent the infection from spreading.

The Vietnam War was in full swing. Lying in her bed in the hospital tent, Chuen could hear the cannons booming from the south. The hospital was jammed with wounded. So on the transfer report the doctor wrote:

Acute infection from injury. Local tissue necrosis. Situation under control. Sent back to Shanghai for further treatment.

I accompanied Chuen to the Ninth Shanghai People's Hospital. The surgeon unwrapped her left hand. Chuen was relaxed, but my scalp tingled—the inside of her palm had been completely carved away. Gray tendons, yellow fat, even some white bones were exposed.

"Doesn't it look like a radio with the back open?" Chuen joked.

The doctor finished the examination, cut off the remaining dead tissue, and applied sulfanilamide paste. Then he rewrapped the hand.

"You're damn lucky," he said to Chuen, "that those army doctors didn't saw off your whole arm."

"Maybe too many teeth had broken off the saw," Chuen said. "You never know how many bullets and how much shrapnel are stuck in those bones."

The doctor chuckled.

"I think it's your optimistic nature that saved you," he said, patting Chuen's shoulder. "But I must tell you the truth. I can heal your wound, but I can't bring the function back to these fingers. You've lost too much. Muscle, tendons, blood vessels, nerve, too much is missing. I'm sorry to say that, in the future, your radio is only for display."

Every other day Chuen went to have her dressing changed. Three months later the wound had healed. The scar tissue shrank, pulling the withered fingers downward, like a chicken claw. The hospital ended her treatment and concluded:

FUNCTION OF THE LEFT HAND HAS BEEN LOST.

Chuen brought the hospital document to the district government office that administered the campaign to settle students in the countryside. In her interview the official kept asking Chuen questions, obviously suspecting that we had some "backdoor" connections at the hospital. My sister became impatient. She unwrapped the gauze and shoved her injured hand right under his nose. Almost immediately, an official seal was stamped on the paper.

Then we had to deal with the red tape from the rubber plantation in Yunnan. After our experiences in the district government office, Chuen and I went to a photography studio to have a picture taken of her hand. It was the same studio where our family portrait had been made twelve years before, and I thought the photographer was the same one, too. He had once flirted with my little sister and gotten her to open her lips in a smile, but he was unable to flirt her shrunken fingers open this time.

Chuen sent the picture of her hand to the rubber plantation along with all sorts of official documents. Readily and briskly, the plantation agreed to transfer Chuen's residency registration to Shanghai. They were smart. There was an abundance of youths with two healthy hands; why should they burden themselves with a defective girl?

Chuen's residency registration was accepted by Shanghai. In the box reserved for the reason for moving back there was one word:

CRIPPLED

As I write this, I feel a prickling on the back of my neck.

My parents once tried to change their children's fate by using lye. A dozen years later, without knowing of their plot, I resorted to the same medium, continuing their unfinished scheme. And I succeeded. I succeeded in changing my sister's fate—from a healthy girl to a lifelong cripple.

In the twelve or thirteen years after Chuen's accident, along with the quenching of the battle fires of the Indochina War, the climate of southern Yunnan cooled considerably. More than half of the plantation's rubber trees succumbed to cold, froze, and died. The remaining trees were sickly; only a few drops could be squeezed out of each trunk, and the sap always dried before it reached the collection bucket.

The plantation tried to switch to cultivating rice, but the harvest could hardly outweigh the seeds. The steep slopes and thin soil were blamed. Then it tried an orchard. A local joke described the results:

With the fruit harvested from the orchard, the local officials feasted their superior, who came to inspect the new experiment.

"Wow!" The senior officer was impressed. "These pears are pretty big!"

"Th-thank you, sir," the host stuttered. "But they are actually watermelons."

"Oh, excuse me." The inspector turned to another platter on the table. "These grapes are really eye-catchers!"

"They are pears, sir."

This time monkeys and hornbills were the scapegoats.

But according to my sister Chuen, nature was not solely responsible for the farm's misfortunes. She told me an anecdote that summed up the prevailing morale during the last few declining years of the plantation.

At the beginning of the rainy season, the boys in Chuen's company were assigned to spread fertilizer on the upper rice paddies. Each boy hoisted a sack of chemical fertilizer onto his back and headed for the hills. The sacks were heavy, and the boys took a break beside a drainage ditch. They looked around, and saw that no officers were watching. Then they decided to take a "short cut"—they cut the threads that bound the tops of the sacks. Grabbing his bag from the bottom, each boy gave a heave. The whole caravan's load of white powder was dumped into the ditch. But the boys saved the sacks—made of sturdy cloth, they were fine bonuses for the day's hard work.

The fog obscured their maneuver; the stream carried away the evidence. Yet later, the reeds along the ditch grew strikingly tall and thick. A luxurious green belt wound down the hill, circling among the paddies dotted with retarded rice seedlings.

But the boys had their trophies. Some of them asked their girlfriends to tailor the fertilizer sacks into shorts—in the front, bold letters labeled the crotch "Pure Urea"; on the butt, a warning: "Use no Hooks."

A string of failures eroded the plantation's sense of mission, and gradually paralyzed the farm. Although each morning the loudspeakers still loyally blasted a splendid reveille to usher in the tropical sun, thousands of workers had nothing to do but attend meetings all day. But even if all you did was study Chairman Mao's quotations of great wisdom, you still had to eat. Truckload after truckload of food was brought in, but nothing came back out. Yunnan Province could not tolerate it any longer. At last the decision to disband was made. The ex-students, now in their thirties, finally returned to their original cities.

Those once peach-fresh girls, after many years' struggle on the southern border, came home to Shanghai. Facing the fact that they didn't have many prime years left, their urgent concern became starting a family. Every day after work they hastily patted powder on their faces, trying to cover their crow's-feet, and rushed to meet that evening's prospective husband.

But Chuen had married way ahead of them, and now she had a daughter. Her husband was a farmer in the suburbs. Chuen's left hand was only for show, but her Shanghai residency was the genuine article. According to government policy, children's residency was determined by their mother's location. From her very first wail, Chuen's daughter was a city resident! The down-to-earth farmer-husband was very proud of his daughter's speedy luck.

One day, Chuen and I were alone in the attic, and we talked about the accident.

"Tell me the truth," I asked her, "did you ever have any regrets about the whole thing?"

Silence.

"I mean . . ." I was trying to soften my aggressiveness when Chuen abruptly asked:

"Remember the abortion?"

"What? What abortion?"

"Sorry, I lost you. Time really flies. I mean, before I came back, did the girl tell you about the abortion, the public abortion at the Third Battalion?"

"Oh, yeah."

"Did you ever wonder how they restrained the girl so they could do it?"

I held my breath, waiting for the answer.

"A stick," Chuen said. "They tied her knees to the ends of a stick. Her legs were stretched wide open."

I coughed.

Chuen, however, looked indifferent. She was telling a story about a third person. It was history.

"But let's face it," I continued to press my sister, "even without that accident you would have been back by now."

"Who knows?" Chuen replied.

"You're not picky; I am sure you wouldn't have starved to death," I joked. "And you had a great collection of snakebite remedies, didn't you?"

"Let me tell you something," Chuen said. "Every time I went to the commander's office, I first stashed a knife in my blouse."

In this chapter, I related quite a few anecdotes about the southern territory. The apparent purpose is to provide the reader with historical facts. But I know that it is really in self-defense. I am trying, over and over again, to defend my deeds. But all my rationalizing does not acquit my sins.

More than twenty years have passed since my sister was crippled. Yet the scene in my first wet dream still appears again and again, in different versions and with different twists. The toes that clamp my body are no longer pink or soft or warm. Sometimes they look like a huge chain, scabbed over with rust. Sometimes they appear as gigantic lizards' necks with rattling scales.

My American roommate has been awakened by my screams many times. He suggested that I seek help from a counselor at school—it was free and confidential. But I didn't go. I knew I had committed a crime. I am suffering the punishment I deserve. No one can help me.

I feel guilty about the doctors who rescued and treated my sister. I assume I fooled them simply because they never thought about the human mind as being more dangerous than tetanus. Sometimes I even get a feeling that those experienced doctors may never have been fooled at all. Perhaps they intentionally left a corner of the net open, giving my sister a way out.

When I first read about Dr. Jack Kevorkian, who invented and marketed a suicide machine to help terminally ill patients end their lives, I felt sort of relieved. In this world, I thought, finally there is someone who shares my mentality and morality. But on further reflection, I found it difficult to quote that case in my defense. Dr. Kevorkian's purpose was to end the meaningless suffering of the dying patient. Though my sister was suffering, she was far from despair. I had no right to impose my own desperation on her. I abused her trust in her brother.

Since the middle toe on my right foot withered, I have not gone barefoot or worn sandals. Polished leather shoes hide well the ugliness curled in the dark. But sometimes when I hold a delicate, diamond-ringed hand and dance in the dim light of a chandelier, I get a sudden chill—on the other side of the earth it is morning, and my sister is rushing to work, swinging her shrunken hand.

I have read reports about the Nazis' experiments on the human body in their concentration camps. Those German army doctors are still the targets of organizations hunting for war criminals. I have often felt that I am being hunted, too, hunted by my own conscience.

The Nazi doctors must have had their glorious reasons to justify their brutality: nation, mankind, science. Their actions are nonetheless condemned by history. I even think that if I had been one of those Nazi doctors, I would quite probably have actively participated and made a significant contribution. I know I am a cold-blooded person, with a ferocious nature.

I am now fifty years old. I know that I will continue to be hunted for decades, hunted until the end of my life. Fortunately, I am an atheist. Once I die, the case is closed. Nobody will be able to hunt me anymore.

CHAPTER THIRTY-FOUR

No Armband

At dawn on a winter morning in 1976, Father died. Curling his body on his pallet, leaving a patch of saliva on his pillow, Father quietly passed away.

Around noontime I went to the local police office to report his death. Father died in November. That meant that his ration coupons for the rest of the year, December, had to be turned back in. The coupons included allotments of twenty-nine pounds of rice, a half-pound of oil, one pound of sugar, one pound of eggs, one pound of meat, one pound of fish, a half-pound of soybean products, one piece of soap, one box of matches, and five packs of cigarettes. Father did not smoke, and we always privately traded the cigarette coupons for rice. Fortunately, we had not made the last trade yet. A death certificate would not be issued until the coupons were submitted. Without a death certificate, the crematorium workers would not come to collect the body.

The next afternoon, the crematorium's hearse stopped at our

door. As usual, a swarm of kids surrounded it to watch. As usual, they held their noses and breathed through their fingers, filtering out any suspect germs that were trying to enter their mouths.

The two attendants looked at the death certificate I handed to them, and they put the stretcher back in the truck. I knew they were just following regulations. I had seen the notices hung on both sides of the funeral hall by the revolutionary committee of the crematorium. The posters clearly stated the rules:

The deceased who belonged to any of the Five Black Categories are not permitted the privileges of being carried by stretcher, cosmetic retouching, and funeral ceremonies.

Their ashes may not be collected.

Their family members may not wear armbands during mourning.

Father was dead, but the box listing political status on the death certificate still clearly labeled him as a landlord, the worst of the black categories.

Descending the staircase, the front attendant clutched Father's legs; the attendant behind grabbed Father's arms. As the old saying goes, "A man out of breath is like a stone out of water—dead weight." Father was big and the staircase was narrow. The two young attendants panted all the way down. They didn't complain or swear; perhaps they felt a little guilty that they could not carry Father on a stretcher. They only clenched their teeth and struggled to drag my father down the stairs. The back of Father's head struck every step on the way down, producing a dull, heavy thumping.

Father was dragged feet first up into the truck. His padded

cotton coat bunched high above his waist, exposing his stomach. Father's mouth hung half-open and the back of his head pressed against the corrugated sheet iron of the truck's floor. The attendant was about to close the door when Bao, who had been watching emotionlessly, suddenly yanked off his woolen cap and rushed forward. Blocking the door with his elbow, Bao lifted Father's bald head and jerked the cap on over the skull.

Mother did not come down from the attic.

It was around five o'clock and already getting dark. Bao, Chuen, and I stood on the sidewalk watching the hearse drive away. Father disappeared forever.

What was the big deal about using or not using a stretcher? The stretcher was so grimy I'd bet it hadn't been washed for decades. The dead body lying on it would be lucky to escape without being inflicted with sores everywhere. The privilege of make-up was even more ridiculous—a few strokes of cheap rouge applied to the cheeks and lips, leaving the ears looking even greener.

I had attended the funerals of a few of the workers in my factory. There was a loudspeaker hanging in each funeral hall in the crematory. The loudspeaker was controlled by a pull chain. One twitch, and the standard dirge was provided. Five minutes for ten dollars. Abruptly begun and abruptly ended. The mourning music was a monotonous loop anyway.

Once the girl who monitored the funeral hall cut off the music ahead of time. The union chairman from our factory, who was presiding at the service, walked up to the girl and negotiated with her. He talked patiently to her, offering analogies like "If you go to a market to buy meat and the butcher doesn't give you the full pound, how do you feel? If you . . ." The girl just ignored him and continued spitting sunflower seed hulls on the floor. Finally, she couldn't stand the old man's endless nagging any longer.

"Cut it out!" She flounced over to the loudspeaker. "I'll give you another two minutes, okay?" With a tug, the solemn music reentered, and all the heads were relowered.

As for the ashes, I once detoured to the furnace room to take a look. The room was neat and clean. There were five furnaces standing in a row. But under the grating of each furnace was a thick deposit of white ashes. Once a body was burnt, the operator would casually scoop some of the ashes into a red silk bag. He tied the bag closed, gave it a slap, and the job was done. The name of the deceased was written on the bag. A portrait of the dead person could be drawn on the mahogany box that held the bag; just don't ask who the hell was inside.

After Father died, I joked about these things often, and I laughed often. Even Mother couldn't help but chuckle as she wiped away her tears.

We didn't violate any regulations. No funeral. No flowers. No ashes. No armbands. Everything went smoothly, with no unexpected consequences. Only the armband issue caused a bit of trouble later for my sister.

Around a year after Father died, my sister's father-in-law passed away. His political status was "Poor Peasant," one of the mainstays of the revolution. In the countryside funerals are taken very seriously. The family bought dozens of yards of black silk for armbands.

Chuen did not go to the funeral, giving the excuse that she was not well. Only after a week had passed did she go to the countryside to spend time with her mother-in-law.

According to the customs of the area, relatives wore the black armbands for at least three months. But Chuen never wore one, not even once. Her simpleminded husband pleaded with her until he ran out of spit. But his wife, cooing with her newborn daughter, pretended not to hear a word and gave no explanation. My brother-in-law complained about the incident for a long time afterward. Every time he started an argument, he began his grumbling with:

"Armband! You didn't even wear an armband . . ."

More than ten years have passed since Father died. In those ten years the situation in China has eased considerably. Revolutionary committees and the posters in the crematorium have dissipated like the smoke from the furnaces. Terms such as the Five Black Categories have gradually faded away.

Mother grew old. She was so old that she could no longer get up from her bed. Chuen sent a tape to me in Vermont. She said that Mother could not write anymore but had urgent things to tell me. Maybe it was a bad recording, or maybe it was because all her teeth were gone—Mother's voice was garbled throughout the message. On the tape she repeated herself over and over again before I could finally understand.

"Long-long," Mother said, "when I die, if you can come back, you children can only see me off at the door. Remember, no funeral. Remember, no ashes. Remember, no armband. Long-long . . ."

Mother, I heard you. But your son is in a distant land, far, far away. I'm afraid I cannot stand on the sidewalk to see you off. But I will remember your words—no armband.

CHAPTER THIRTY-FIVE

I Slapped My Sister

In June of 1976 I married. My wife's name is Yifei; she is six years younger than I. Yifei was the only girl who climbed up to the attic more than once. Sometimes I even got the feeling that our attic was a forbidden altar like the pagoda that I lured Wang Tian to many years ago. As a result of her adventurous, rebellious decision, my wife suffered in many ways in the following years.

The Shanghainese say, "It is easier to find a bride than to find a house." On first hearing, this seems to be desecration of human dignity. But think it over and it does have a flavor of Marxist materialism—the heat and pressure needed to make a brick is much greater than that needed to court a woman. In my case, finding a wife was not easy, but finding a house was even harder.

My wife and I lived separately for a year and a half after we were married. She still lived with her parents; I still lived in the attic. We became a "walking couple"—taking a walk together every day. Movie theaters and bushes in parks continued to be our shelters for necking. And we grabbed any chance we could to sleep together for one night or a few hours. We always carried our marriage certificate with us—in case anybody raised questions about our "inappropriate behavior."

I tried to persuade her to move into the attic, but Yifei declined. She said it was inconvenient for two families to live in such a space. Be patient, we'll have our own home sooner or later, she insisted.

We developed the habit of browsing in furniture shops. Amid the fragrances of lacquer and wax, we fantasized about different decors and arrangements for our future home.

I still believe that Yifei would be much better off if she had married someone else. She did have many choices—she was astonishingly beautiful. Tall, slender, fair, she had a complexion as translucent as white Italian marble. And her demeanor had a touch of marble-like coldness.

I always wonder why Yifei chose me. Even Yifei herself could not explain her strange resolution. Her father was a fabric designer before the revolution. Though not in the mainstream of the new regime, artists were regarded as allies of the revolution—a status far superior to my father's. And Yifei had a decent job. She was a quality inspector in a state-run woolen mill that manufactured sweaters exclusively for export. After ten years cut off from the world, only a few Chinese factories did business with foreigners. A touch of the glamour from products destined for the Western market seemed to rub off onto the workers in those export factories.

Yifei handed in an application to the personnel director in her factory, asking for permission to marry. The whole conversation lasted less than five minutes, Yifei told me.

"I bet you know his family's background already," the director said, tapping on the application form. "Am I right?"

"Yes, you are right." Yifei answered.

"According to the marriage laws of the People's Republic of China, you are free to marry anybody you want," the director took a sip of her tea. "But I have to tell you that our factory has very high expectations of you."

"Thank you very much."

"We are looking forward to you playing a much more important role in the future. You are valuable to our factory."

"That's very nice of you."

"And also according to the marriage laws, nobody can force you into a marriage that is against your free will. Are you aware of this right?"

"Yes, I am aware of this right."

"Then, do you have any second thoughts about your application?"

"No."

Like most of our generation, Yifei was brought up and educated as an atheist. I have no idea where she got the eerie spiritual notions that wandered through her mind. She once told me that, after she married me, the same nightmare that had haunted her since she was very young ceased to reoccur. She said she had dreamed for years that she hanged herself on a tree covered with white flowers.

One night, dozing beside me, she murmured, "It must have had something to do with my previous life."

"Nonsense," I said.

She rolled over. Facing me, arching back her long and beautiful neck, she showed me a faint red trail around her throat.

"It has been there since I was born," she said.

Our son came into the world. My wife finally gave in and, carrying our baby, moved into the attic. She gave up the wardrobe, gave up the dresser, the lamp, and the sofa. She only asked for a bed. Her least requirement was an unrealistic luxury in the attic—in thirty years, my family had never had a bed. But we were touched by her dedication and sincerity. With a tape measure Chuen, her husband, and I checked every corner of the attic. With the accuracy and tolerance of a piston and its cylinder, we placed a bed under the north window—two inches were sawed off each leg.

A bed is only a bed. The important thing was that three people had to fit on the platform. The procedure for filling the space between ceiling and bed was as follows:

Step 1.   The son is laid flat on the outer edge of the bed and gently pushed to the inside, where the bed meets the ceiling.

Step 2.   The wife lies flat on her back and, using her shoulder muscles, wriggles to the center of the bed.

Step 3.   The husband lies down, filling the rest of the area.

Step 4.   The curtain is pulled closed.

At this point the triangular space was packed solid.

My son would poke his fingers into the knotholes of the ceiling for a while and then fall asleep. If we had the inclination, Yifei and I could lie on our sides and explore the heavens together. The classical Chinese called those things "fog and dew." Well said. Fog and dew, absolutely quiet. During the following two years, we were very quiet; even the bed boards did not squeak.

At the other end of the attic there was another curtain. Behind the curtain, four more people lay on the southern pallet: Mother, Chuen, her husband, and their infant daughter. The only noise that escaped from behind that curtain was the occasional crying of the baby.

Chuen and I had both grown up in the attic. Those beams and walls had become organic parts of our bodies; we never felt cramped. But since Yifei moved in, the attic had evolved into a problem.

Starting with the block committee and working our way up through the district government, the municipal government, and ultimately, the State Department of the People's Republic of China, my sister and I wrote an unceasing stream of letters, pleading with them to solve our housing problem.

No response. The whole appeals campaign had been a monologue. We quit.

Mother was over seventy by then. She remained essentially healthy, but walking was growing more difficult for her day by day. She still managed, however, to get to market to sell cubes of ginger and small bunches of scallions.

Every time she returned from the market, Mother labored to climb the staircase with her basket. She paused at every third step, but she did not sit down—if she sat, she could no longer get back up. She would rest the basket on a higher step and lean on it with both hands. In the attic we could hear her panting when she was still on the first floor. Mother would allow us to carry the basket for her, but she wouldn't tolerate our helping her up the stairs. She said she wasn't that old and she could manage by herself.

Climbing up to the attic was difficult, but descending was even tougher. Mother could no longer walk downstairs facing forward; she had to turn around and climb down like a toddler. We asked her to quit the scallion and ginger business, but she said it was a good workout, anyway.

Mother continued to dabble in her last and smallest enterprise for about a year, but one evening she hung her half-basket of scallions in front of the window, where it remained for almost five days. Each morning Mother covered the scallions with a damp cloth to keep them from drying out, but the scallions began to rot. Mother picked out the slimy rotting pieces each evening, hoping to return to the market the next day. But she was never able to climb down from the attic again. Eventually, she asked Chuen to buy a few pounds of fish and then cooked up a big pot of carp with scallions. The scaliions are usually just a seasoning in the dish, but this time Mother put in all her leftovers. The carp hid in the thick weeds, and there was no way to find them. From then on, Mother gave up and began what she called "life as a zombie."

Mother could no longer work and yet she unexpectedly became our trump card.

In the late 1970s, China's policy toward Taiwan underwent an abrupt change. Slogans like "We must liberate Taiwan!" and

"Rescue the Taiwanese people from hellfire!" which had been splashed on walls all over the country for almost thirty years were quietly painted over. The new policy enthusiastically and emotionally called for Taiwan to "come back to the mother-land." The hatred that was the result of decades of bloody civil war evaporated overnight. The battle that had cost millions of lives was now nostalgically remembered as a squabble between naughty children.

One evening as we finished our dinner, we heard a knock at the door. It was an official who said he was there on behalf of the Shanghai Government's Office of Taiwan Reunification.

"Do you have a younger brother named Lai Ling living in Taiwan?" the official asked my mother.

"Yes," Mother replied.

"Is your brother a senior officer in the Taiwanese air force?"

"I know nothing about his situation now. We haven't written to each other for almost forty years," Mother said. "I only re-member that in World War II he was a pilot, and shot down quite a few Japanese planes."

"Your brother has a son working in the United Nations, right?"

"The last time I saw him, his son was still breast-feeding. I know nothing about what happened after that."

"Your brother's son recently wrote a letter to our govern-ment, asking permission to visit China," the official said. "He is looking for you."

Mother burst into tears.

The official encouraged my mother to correspond with her brother in Taiwan and to tell him of our family's happy life. He said the reunification of the country was everybody's business. When he had finished his talk, he looked around.

"Your house is a little crowded, isn't it?" he commented.

We didn't say anything.

Give me a break, I thought, what the heck does the reunification of Taiwan have to do with our attic? To our astonishment, however, four days after the official's visit, Mother received a note from the district's housing administration. The note said that a new apartment was reserved for my mother. We immediately rushed over to see the apartment. It was a three-room suite—bedroom, living room, and kitchen, plus a flush toilet!

But now, Chuen and I faced a dilemma—who would move with Mother and who would stay in the attic? The apartment was registered in Mother's name so she had to be the one to make the decision.

For the next few days, Chuen and I were very polite to each other. We wanted to say something, but didn't know what to say. Sometimes our eyes met and we would quickly look away. We acted like we had done something shameful.

Every night, Mother sighed behind the curtain.

One day about a week later, when no one else was in the attic, Mother called Chuen and me to her side. Mother said she thought it would be more convenient for her to live with Chuen's family.

I was furious. I accused Chuen of plotting behind my back. Chuen jumped to her feet and said that was bullshit. I swung my arm and slapped her. Chuen staggered and almost fell down. She reached for support from the table and hit the corner with her wounded palm. It hurt so much that she doubled over, cold sweat breaking out on her forehead. I yanked open the trapdoor and ran out.

I didn't come back for several days; I slept at the factory. Finally I got a call from my wife. She said that Mother had talked with Chuen and they had decided to let my family move to the new apartment with Mother.

Chuen and her husband helped me to move. Bao came to lend a hand, too. They were all very happy. They cracked jokes and laughed. I made jokes, too, but I felt my laugh was laughable. I had to concentrate on my facial muscles the whole time.

Mother let me move first, saying she would come later.

But she never came.

A few months later her nephew came to China. He was the director of the Asia Department, United Nations Development Program (UNDP).

Mother met him in the attic.

Chuen called to ask me over to the attic for a family reunion feast, but I didn't go.

CHAPTER THIRTY-SIX

Farewell

In 1979, fifteen years after I started working in the factory, I began to write. To my surprise, my first few short stories attracted disproportionate attention. From that time on, my career gradually shifted from engineering to literature.

In the summer of 1987 I received a full scholarship to Middlebury College in Vermont. The very evening I got my visa from the U.S. consulate in Shanghai, I went to the attic to say good-bye to my mother and sister.

Since my family moved to the new apartment, I seldom went back to my old home. I could make plenty of excuses for my absence, but every time I passed by Penglai Road, I couldn't help but lift my head and look at the north window of the attic.

When I lived there, I often forgot to bring my keys and couldn't get in the front door. So I would stand across the street and lift my head toward the north window of the attic and yell:

"O-p-e-n the d-o-o-r!"

When Mother was still healthy and heard me calling, she would yell back from high up in the attic:

"I'-m c-o-m-i-n-g!"

Then I would stand on the sidewalk and listen through the door. I would hear her slow, heavy tread coming down the staircase, one step after another.

When Chuen returned to Shanghai from the plantation, she was usually the one to come down and open the door for me. Her tread was completely different from Mother's. It sounded like strafing from a machine gun, rescuing me from street muggings.

It was drizzling the evening I went to the attic for the last time. I stood across the street, lifted my head, and looked at the north window. The window was closed; the light was on. One of the glass panes was broken; a piece of board had been nailed over the hole.

I cleared my throat and stretched out my neck. Like a wolf, I called:

"O-p-e-n the d-o-o-r!"

The road was empty. My voice sounded strange to me. Had I really been calling like that for more than thirty years? I crossed the street and stood beside the door, listening. I was hoping to hear the familiar footfalls, but I didn't hear anything.

I was about to call again, when the door quietly opened. Standing in the dark doorway, Chuen silently looked at me. I tried to say hello, but only a half-strangled noise escaped from my throat. Chuen turned away and started upstairs. I followed my sister, the steps squeaking under my feet.

There had been few changes in the attic. The bed had been removed. The curtain was gone; only the curtain wire still stretched loosely along the beam. A pair of tiny socks was clipped to the wire.

"Where's the little devil?" I managed to ask in a relaxed tone.

"Her father took her out to play," Chuen answered in a plain voice, as plain as cold tofu.

Chuen sat on the south pallet with her legs crossed. Beside her, the pallet was empty. I was shocked.

"Where's Mom?" I asked.

"She went to Xian. Ling brought Mother to his place for a visit."

"How did you get her down the stairs?"

"We managed."

My heart felt hollow. I couldn't say anything.

Face to face, Chuen and I sat on the pallet. We each looked at our own knees. We could hear each other's breathing.

A cricket called.

Somewhere on the roof, weak and trembling, it sounded like a baby crying far away.

It was the earliest cricket of the year. By the middle of fall, I knew, the whole roof would be jubilant with the singing of the cricket choir. But I would not hear them anymore.

"I'm going away," I said in a low voice and waited for her questions. But Chuen did not ask. I had to continue on my own.

"I'm leaving for the United States."

Chuen remained silent.

"I'm going to study, to attend college over there," I murmured. "I don't know when I can come back again."

"Is everything set?" Chuen finally spoke.

"Yes, everything is set."

"What about your wife and son?"

"They can't go now."

"By sea or by air?"

"Air."

"Did you buy the ticket?"

"Not yet. I'm still short of money. But it won't be a problem; I'll have enough in a few weeks."

Chuen turned her back, crawled into the corner, and opened a trunk. She took out an envelope and handed it to me. It was heavy. I opened the envelope—a wad of money.

"I've heard that everything is very expensive over there. Bring extra clothes with you. Daddy hoped all his life that we'd have a college student in our family. You three boys were beaten too much. Daddy seemed to be trying to whack a college student out of you. It wasn't your fault. You didn't deserve punishment," Chuen's voice was a little choked. "Finally you've made good. Daddy can rest easy in hell."

"I want to go to Xian to see Mom before I go."

"Forget about that!" Chuen slapped her knee.

Abruptly, I heard Father slamming on the table. Twenty years ago, during the relocation, Father and Mother were sending their sons to be recruited. That morning, Father shouted at Ling and me. Chuen was still playing under the table then; she couldn't possible remember Father's desperation. But a couple of decades later, Chuen yelled out exactly the same words, and wore Father's exact expression.

I shivered.

"You know the situation here better than me. It could change any time," Chuen's breath quickened. "Leave, leave as soon as possible!"

In the dim light, beads of sweat gleamed on Chuen's forehead. "Don't worry about the family. Yifei and I will take care of each other. Do you hear me?"

"Yes, I hear you."

The clock chimed.

It was Father's clock. As it chimed it squeaked.

Seven o'clock.

"Long-long," Chuen pointed at my right foot and said, "take that sock off, will you?"

I didn't know what she meant, but I obediently took the sock off my right foot. The shrunken middle toe was exposed.

Chuen took the glove off her left hand, revealing her shrunken fingers. She bent over and reached out her hand toward my foot.

The claw-like fingers and the claw-like toe approached each other, closer and closer.

They touched.

A Boeing-727 zoomed into the air. On August 24, the third day after I got my visa, I flew to the United States.

Compositor: G & S Typesetters, Inc.
Text: 11/15 Granjon
Display: Bernhard Modern
Printer: Haddon Craftsmen
Binder: Haddon Craftsmen

DUE

201-6503

Printed
in USA